the authorized

INTERNATIONAL ASSOCIATION OF COOKING SCHOOLS

C·O·O·K·B·O·O·K

THE INTERNATIONAL ASSOCIATION OF COOKING SCHOOLS

C·O·O·K·B·O·O·K

IRENA CHALMERS COOKBOOKS INC. ◆ NEW YORK

IRENA CHALMERS COOKBOOKS, INC.

PUBLISHER
Irena Chalmers

Sales and Marketing Director
Diane J. Kidd

Managing Editor
Jean Atcheson

Editor for this book
Helen Scott-Harman

Cover Design
Milton Glaser, Inc.

Cover Photography
Matthew Klein

Interior Design
Linn Fischer
Dorothy Atcheson

Typesetting
Acu-Type, Inc., Clinton, Connecticut

Printing
Bason Associates, Graham, North Carolina

Editorial Offices
23 East 92nd Street
New York, NY 10028
(212) 289-3105

Sales Offices
P.O. Box 322
Brown Summit, NC 27214
(919) 656-3115

ISBN #0-941034-14-3
©1981 by the International Association of Cooking Schools.
All rights reserved. Printed and published in the
United States of America by Irena Chalmers Cookbooks, Inc.
LIBRARY OF CONGRESS
CATALOG CARD NO.: 81-70440
  International Association of Cooking Schools Cookbook
  Greensboro, NC: Chalmers, Irena Cookbooks
  200 p.
  8110   811007

I am delighted to have this opportunity to greet the cooking school community and all those interested in the International Association of Cooking Schools; at the same time, it is my great pleasure to commend the many members who have contributed so valuably to this splendid and useful collection of recipes.

As you undoubtedly know, a steadily burgeoning interest in good cooking — not only in the United States, of course, but all over the world — has prompted a phenomenal growth in the number and kinds of cooking schools that offer students instruction of the first quality. Our Association was founded in 1978 expressly to link these schools in a network designed to promote the vitality of mutual support in our highly creative field. This book, the result of an artful collaboration within the Association, is happy evidence of the success of our original hopes.

In the Association, cooking teachers today enjoy a forum for the lively exchange of ideas and information, and the encouragement and mutual support that are the natural rewards of open communication. In this continuing dialogue, we are able to reinforce our commitments to the highest standards in teaching, in the pursuit of culinary knowledge and in ethical conduct.

The Association's voluntary certification program for cooking teachers — the first of its kind to be introduced in the United States — was designed by our Standards Committee, was overwhelmingly accepted by our membership, and is now being implemented. While the program quite rightly and appropriately recognizes the diversity among cooking teachers in matters of style and technique, this first-level certification provides uniform basic requirements in education, in teaching experience, in the knowledge of food and cooking and all fields related, and in extent of participation in the activities of the Association.

The eight standing committees of the International Association of Cooking Schools form the backbone of our organization, and each makes important contributions to our overall aims in communication, education and the maintenance of professional standards. Projects include a bi-monthly newsletter; the study of the contents of food products; the processing and labeling of foods; and workshops on food and business-related topics.

We meet annually in the spring, an occasion which is the culmination of committee efforts and the high point of the Association year. Cooking colleagues have the opportunity then to learn and instruct in formal seminars and informal meetings. Then, as well as in special classes, on tours and at social events, the infectious enthusiasm of the members is easy to recognize as the Association's real strength and greatest enduring stimulus.

These are the fine cooks and fine teachers whose creativity colors and enlivens this book, and makes it such a valuable resource for school and kitchen. We hope that it will help you at home and perhaps may inspire you to consider taking classes soon with one of our member cooking teachers (a list of their names appears at the back of the book) as you continue to expand your culinary horizons.

Richard E. Nelson
President
International Association of Cooking Schools

♦ MESSAGE FROM THE COOKBOOK COMMITTEE CHAIRMAN ♦

Our aim from the beginning of this project was to produce a collection of recipes that would fairly represent the entire cooking school community, and I am pleased to find that this is what we have achieved. In serving the needs of both home and career cooking students, our members teach thousands of classes every week. Their influence extends well beyond the classroom, through special demonstrations, articles, industry consultations, catering and gourmet retail consultation. Through this book, their expertise can bring benefits to a wider audience than ever before.

For this achievement, I want to thank particularly the members of the Cookbook Committee, who have worked so diligently and enthusiastically:

Shirley and Arch Corriher
Charlotte Ann Albertson
Karen Benner
Rubye Erickson
Irene Rothschild
Patricia Tabibian

I give special thanks as well to George Munger, a member of the board of our Association who advised our committee; to Mary Hibbits, our executive vice president, for her many hours of consultation and help; to our publisher, Irena Chalmers, for her long-standing support of this project; and to Helen Scott-Harman, the hands-on editor of these many pages.

Anne Byrd

Anne Byrd
Chairman
Cookbook Committee
International Association of Cooking Schools

CONTENTS

CONTENTS

CONTENTS

CONTENTS

CONTENTS

"America might well be leading and nurturing the explosion of interest in food that has marked the last decade."

— Julia Child,
in her keynote speech to the annual meeting of the
International Association of Cooking Schools,
March 21, 1981

It is appropriate, if not inevitable, that such a book as this be produced in America, although coming from an organization that is international in scope. For, as Julia Child also observed, "No other country has an organization of this type."

It is probably redundant to say that this is a very big cookbook — its heft is already apparent in your hand — but with that observation comes no apology. To be a really comprehensive representation of our community of master cooks, it has to be big.

An advantage of bigness, in this instance, is the range it accommodates, which enables the reader to shop these pages as a kind of adventure — a Moroccan souk could not offer a more colorful and abundant variety of temptations. Nor is there any process suggested here that is beyond the abilities of the interested and diligent cook.

One way to use these sections is as a series of private master classes, taken at your option and to fit your schedule. In this book the masters disclose their attitudes, their methods — many never before published — and their techniques, material hitherto available only through discussion in class. Browse here at your leisure, and follow any attractive path with confidence. The effort here has been to simplify and clarify. None of our contributors wishes to overwhelm you; all want to help you to achieve confidence as well as excellence.

Recognizing the disparity in approaches and techniques among our contributors, the editors have carefully codified the variables, so that while the recipes are wonderfully different from one another, the expression of them is uniform, so that together they form a coherent whole.

It is important to remember that the careful choice of fresh and good ingredients will be crucial to the successful realization of your hopes for any of these recipes. Poor quality in raw materials cannot be compensated for by any amount of technique; a wise eye at the market comes first, before the happy labor in the kitchen.

Hors d'Oeuvres

The recipes in this section make appropriate foods for sociability, particularly any cocktail setting. The quantity of each one, offered alone, is usually sufficient to serve six people at drinks. Make three kinds and you'll have enough for a party of 20. Five kinds will serve 40. Or — if you feel like it — just increase the quantity of all the recipes in this section and invite everybody you know.

Properly, hors d'oeuvres are foods eaten away from the table, prior to a meal. In French the meaning literally is "outside the work." In this instance, "work" refers to art, not labor.

You will find hors d'oeuvres here for all seasons and from all parts of this country and many foreign ports and capitals. Some, such as the Greek Cheese Puffs, are finger foods. Others are more conveniently eaten in wedges on a plate — Leek Tart, for example, or Salmon Mousse. There are dips here, and meats, vegetables, biscuits, breads and spreads. Many are easy to prepare at the last moment; others recommend themselves to advance preparation, when you have plenty of time. Some can even be converted into mealtime dishes for informal occasions such as Sunday lunch or a midnight supper.

Leek Tart
(Tarte aux Poireaux)

A young fruity Beaujolais goes well with this hors d'oeuvre.

Chez Mimi Cooking School
Mimi Gormezano
Iowa City, Iowa

Serves 8
Preheat oven to 350 degrees

CRUST:
1 cup unbleached flour
¼ pound unsalted butter, cut into small pieces
4 ounces Herkimer cheddar or
    Gruyère cheese, grated
Salt
White pepper

FILLING:
7 tablespoons unsalted butter
1 pound leeks, white part and 1 inch of green
    stems, thinly sliced and washed carefully
Salt
Freshly ground pepper
½ cup heavy cream

1 egg
1 teaspoon cream

Sift the flour into a large bowl and cut in butter with fingertips or a knife or pastry blender until it resembles cornmeal in texture. Add the cheese and salt and pepper to taste. Form the dough into a ball, wrap in plastic wrap and refrigerate for at least half an hour.

Heat half the butter over low heat in a large frying pan that has a tight lid. Add the leeks, cover and cook slowly for about 10 minutes. Add 4 tablespoons of water to the pan, cover and cook another 5 minutes. Add the remaining butter a little at a time. Do not let the leeks brown. Push the leeks to the side of the pan after they have absorbed all the butter and moisture and there is no liquid left in the pan. Add the heavy cream and heat slowly. Season with salt and pepper and keep warm.

Roll out the pastry to ⅛ inch thickness on a floured pastry board, and line a 10-inch tart pan or individual tart pans. Weight the crust and bake for about 10 minutes or until almost cooked. Remove the weights. Prick the bottom and sides. Lightly beat the egg with the cream and paint the pastry with the mixture. Bake for 15 minutes longer until the pastry is lightly browned. Fill the tart crust with the leek mixture and serve hot.

Scallops Seviche

The scallops keep their delicate flavor due to being "cooked" only by the action of lime and lemon juices. To make this, use only top quality olive oil.

Peggy Foreman's Cooking School
Peggy Foreman
Atlanta, Georgia

Serves 8

1 pound bay scallops left whole, or sea scallops, cut into small pieces
¼ cup lime juice
¼ cup lemon juice
½ cup olive oil
1 clove garlic, minced
Salt
White pepper
Parsley to garnish

Wash the scallops carefully to remove all traces of sand. Put the scallops in a glass or ceramic bowl. Add all the remaining ingredients except the parsley and mix well. Refrigerate overnight or leave for about 2 hours at room temperature. Drain and place on a platter with toothpicks. Garnish with parsley. Serve with melba toast.

Snow Peas Tonnato

The tuna dipping sauce should be made well ahead, preferably one, two, or even three days in advance.

Lynne Kasper
Brussels, Belgium

Makes 12-16 servings

2 pounds fresh snow peas, or sugar snap peas
DIPPING SAUCE:
2 cups mayonaise, preferably homemade
1 can (6-7 ounce) tuna, oil packed, well drained
4-6 anchovies, rinsed
3-4 tablespoons chopped onion
2 tablespoons chopped celery
Lemon juice
3-4 tablespoons capers

Wash the peas well and arrange them in a small basket lined with a white napkin. Cover with plastic wrap and refrigerate until serving time.
Combine the mayonnaise, tuna, anchovies, onion and celery in a blender or food processor and blend until smooth. Add the lemon juice to taste. Add the capers and refrigerate for 4 hours before serving.

Greek Cheese Puffs
(Tiropetes)

Marla Horn
Hollywood, Florida

Makes about 100 puffs
Preheat oven to 425 degrees

4 eggs, lightly beaten
1 pound feta cheese, crumbled
1 pound ricotta cheese
4 ounces Swiss cheese, coarsely grated
4 ounces mozarella cheese, coarsely grated
1¼ pounds butter
1 pound filo pastry dough
½ cup oil

Blend together the eggs and cheeses. Melt ¼ pound of the butter and add it to the egg and cheese mixture, stirring well.

Cut the filo pastry into five portions, each approximately 2 inches wide. Wrap four of these in plastic wrap and set aside covered with a damp towel.

Melt the remaining butter and oil together. Remove a thin strip from the block of filo, and brush with the melted butter-oil mixture. Place a scant teaspoon of the cheese mixture in the bottom right corner of the filo strip and fold the left corner over to cover it and form a triangle. Fold again; continue folding, as though folding a flag. End with a triangle shape. Brush this with the butter-oil mixture and place on a baking sheet. Repeat this process until all the filo and the cheese mixture have been used.

Bake in the preheated oven 12 to 15 minutes, or until the puffs are lightly browned. Serve hot.

Ham and Yam Biscuits

Mashed cooked carrots, very well drained, may be substituted for the sweet potato in this recipe.

Frances Neel
White, Georgia

Makes 45 1½-inch biscuits
Preheat the oven to 475 degrees

1⅓ cups self-rising flour
¼ teaspoon baking soda
1 teaspoon baking powder
1 teaspoon sugar
⅔ cup mashed cooked sweet potato
3 tablespoons melted butter
½ cup buttermilk
1 pound country ham, thinly sliced and cut into 1½-inch square pieces

Measure the flour, baking soda, baking powder and sugar into a small bowl and mix with a fork to combine. Blend together the sweet potato, melted butter and buttermilk in a blender or food processor until smooth. Add this mixture to the dry ingredients and stir with a fork until the mixture leaves the sides of the bowl.

Turn out onto a well floured surface and knead gently. Roll out to a thickness of about ½ inch. Cut in 1½-inch rounds using a biscuit cutter.

Bake on a greased cookie sheet 8 to 10 minutes, until well browned. Split and fill with slices of country ham.

Deep-Fried Asparagus

Asparagus spears may be prepared and deep-fried in advance, then refrigerated overnight, covered tightly in foil, then placed in a preheated 400-degree oven for about 10 minutes, until hot and crisp, and served immediately.

Susan Manlin Katzman
Clayton, Missouri

Makes 15 to 20 servings

2 cups sifted flour
1 teaspoon salt
¼ teaspoon pepper
⅓ cup olive oil
1½ cups lukewarm water
5 dozen asparagus spears
Shortening for deep frying
3 egg whites
Salt

Sift the flour, salt and pepper together into a large bowl. Gradually beat in the oil and water with a wire whisk. Beat until the mixture is as smooth and thick as heavy cream. Set aside to rest at room temperature for 2 hours.

Peel and trim the asparagus and wash under cold running water. Heat a large amount of salted water to boiling. Cook the asparagus for 2 minutes; drain and rinse immediately with cold water. Drain well, pat dry and set aside until completely cool.

Heat the shortening slowly to 375 degrees. Beat the egg whites with a pinch of salt until soft peaks are formed. Fold into the batter.

Dip the asparagus spears into the batter and deep fry, a few at a time, for 4-5 minutes until golden brown on all sides. Drain on paper towels. Serve at once or reheat them just before serving.

Carrot-Ginger Quiche

The egg yolk in this crust makes it resistant to moisture without prebaking. Cut into wedges and serve on small plates with forks.

Clay Kitchen at the East Bank
Norma Singleton
South Bend, Indiana

Serves 8 to 10
Preheat oven to 375 degrees

CRUST:
1½ cups unbleached flour
½ cup whole wheat flour
½ teaspoon salt
½ cup unsalted butter
1 egg yolk, beaten
5-7 tablespoons ice water

FILLING:
1½ cups grated carrots
3-4 scallions, chopped
1 tablespoon fresh ginger, grated
1 tablespoon clarified butter
4 eggs, beaten
1½ cups light cream
2 tablespoons sherry
1 teaspoon salt
Pinch of cayenne pepper
5 ounces sharp cheddar cheese, grated

Combine the flours and salt. Cut the butter into the flour with a pastry blender or fork, one tablespoon at a time, until the mixture has the texture of coarse meal. Make a well, and stir in the beaten egg yolk and enough ice water to make the mixture hold together. Form into a ball, and refrigerate for at least half an hour. Roll the dough and fit it into a quiche dish.

Sauté the carrot, scallions and ginger in the clarified butter until soft.

Beat together the eggs, light cream, sherry, salt and cayenne.

Spread the carrot-ginger mixture evenly into the unbaked crust, add the grated cheese, and pour the beaten egg mixture over the cheese.

Bake in the center of the oven for 30 to 35 minutes, until the middle of the quiche is firm and lightly browned. Cool on a wire rack before serving.

Crustless Corn Quiche, Microwave

Quiches with or without crust are quickly made in the microwave oven. This is good served with corn chips or crackers.

Microcookery Center Inc.
Mary Jo Bergland
Glen Ellyn, Illinois

Serves 6 to 8

2 whole jalapeño peppers, chopped
1 small onion, chopped
2 tablespoons butter
Kernels cut from 2 ears fresh sweet corn,
   or 10-ounce package frozen corn
3 eggs, lightly beaten
¾ cup evaporated milk
⅛ teaspoon ground cumin
2 cups shredded Muenster cheese

Combine the peppers, onion and butter in a 1-quart measuring cup and put in the microwave oven. Cook at high for 2 minutes. Add the corn and cook at high for 3 minutes. Stir in the eggs, milk and cumin.

Spread the cheese in a 9-inch quiche dish and pour the custard mixture over the cheese. Cook at high for 9 to 11 minutes, or until set in the center. Rotate the dish twice while it is cooking.

Cold Crudités with Hot Anchovy and Garlic Dip
(Bagna Cauda)

This dip is also good with bread sticks.

Donald S. Luria
Tucson, Arizona

Makes 6 to 8 servings

1 bunch scallions
1 cucumber, peeled and cut in strips
2 carrots, peeled and cut in strips
4 stalks celery, cut in strips
1 sweet red pepper, seeded and cut in strips
1 green pepper, seeded and cut in strips
¾ pound fresh mushrooms
12 cherry tomatoes

DIP:
2 cups heavy cream
4 tablespoons butter
1 can flat anchovy fillets, drained, rinsed and finely chopped
4-6 garlic cloves, finely chopped

Wash the scallions well. Cut each in half after discarding the limp part of the green tops. Put the scallions into a bowl of ice water. Add the cucumber, carrots, celery and peppers. Refrigerate for 1 hour.

Clean the mushrooms. If they are small, leave them whole; if large, cut in halves or quarters. Drain the vegetables, pat dry and arrange them with the mushrooms and tomatoes on a platter. Cover tightly with plastic wrap and refrigerate.

Bring the cream to a boil in a heavy 1-quart enameled or stainless steel saucepan, and cook, stirring frequently, for 15 to 20 minutes, until it has thickened and reduced to about 1 cup.

Meanwhile, heat the butter in a small saucepan over low heat; do not let it brown. Add the anchovies and garlic and simmer for about 5 minutes. Add to the reduced cream, stirring constantly. Heat the mixture just to the simmering point, taking care not to let it boil. Serve hot as a dip for the chilled vegetables.

If the sauce separates after serving, a quick beat with a wire whisk should repair it. It still tastes good after it cools to room temperature, and will keep in the refrigerator, in a sealed jar, for up to 5 days.

Antipasto Spread

This flavorful cheese spread tastes best at room temperature. It is ideally served as the centerpiece of an antipasto platter. Hence its name. It can also be served with crackers, or an array of raw vegetables.

Nancy L. Abrams
Evanston, Illinois

Yields 1½ cups

½ ounce Parmesan cheese, cut in small pieces
2 scallions, washed and cut in 1½-inch slices, including green tops
1 pound ricotta cheese, cut in pieces
¼ teaspoon basil
½ teaspoon salt
Freshly ground pepper

Place the cutting knife into the processor bowl. Cut the Parmesan cheese into ½- to 1-inch pieces. Turn on the processor. Drop one piece of cheese through the feeder tube at a time, immediately followed by another until all the cheese has been added. Continue to run the machine for about 30 seconds, until the cheese has been finely grated. Add the scallions. Turn on the processor and chop the scallions about 10 seconds. Turn off the processor. Add the rest of the ingredients to the bowl. Run the machine for six seconds. Scrape down the side of the bowl. Taste the spread and correct the seasoning. Turn the machine on-off to blend in the additional seasoning.

Brandied Ribs with Brown Mustard Sauce

The S-shaped hooks needed for roasting these spareribs can be found in specialty cooking equipment shops, or you can use curtain hooks. The hoisin sauce is sold in Oriental food shops but is also widely available in supermarkets.

Bobbi Saper
Shawnee Mission, Kansas

Serves 6
Preheat oven to 375 degrees

2 pounds spareribs, cut in half

MARINADE:
¼ cup soy sauce
3 tablespoons honey
2 tablespoons hoisin sauce
1 tablespoon white vinegar
2 cloves garlic, finely chopped
2 tablespoons chicken broth
2 tablespoons sherry
3 tablespoons brandy
2 teaspoons sugar

SAUCE:
1 egg
1 egg yolk
¼ cup white vinegar
2 tablespoons dry mustard
4 tablespoons butter
¼ cup white sugar
¼ cup brown sugar

Trim any excess fat from the spareribs, and remove the overlapping piece of meat on the bony side. Put the spareribs in a long, shallow dish, making sure they lie flat.

Mix together the marinade ingredients and spoon over the ribs. Marinate for 3 hours at room temperature or 6 hours in the refrigerator. Baste ribs frequently and turn them occasionally.

Pierce each rib with an S-shaped hook at one end. Hang them from an oven rack, set in the top position above a drip pan half filled with water. Roast the ribs in the preheated oven for 45 minutes, then raise the temperature to 450 degrees and bake an additional 15 minutes, or until golden brown.

Meanwhile make the sauce: Combine the whole egg and egg yolk with the other ingredients in the top of a double boiler. Cook over boiling water, stirring constantly until the mixture has the consistency of custard. If the sauce begins to separate, beat it until smooth. Chill until ready to serve with the ribs. The sauce will keep well in the refrigerator.

Curried Apple Cheddar Pâté

This is good served with sesame crackers, crisp cucumber slices or celery sticks.

Diana Todd
Newport Beach, California

Yields 3 cups

1 pound curd-style cottage cheese
2 cups finely grated cheddar cheese
1 medium-size cooking apple, peeled, cored and coarsely grated
1 tablespoon curry powder
1 teaspoon salt
Pepper
1 teaspoon finely grated orange peel (optional)

GARNISHES:
1 tablespoon toasted coconut
1 tablespoon chopped walnuts, almonds or other nuts (do not use peanuts)
1 tablespoon thinly sliced stuffed olives
1 tablespoon finely chopped chives or parsley

Beat together the cheeses, apple, curry powder, salt, pepper and the orange peel (if used). Spoon the mixture into a shallow serving bowl and chill until ready to serve.

At serving time, mark a cross on the top of the pâté to divide it into four sections. Press each of the four garnishes onto the surface of one quarter of the pâté.

Yugoslavian Meat Rolls
(Cevapcici)

These small sausage-shaped meat rolls, popular in Yugoslavia, are particularly delicious when grilled over an open fire, but quite satisfactory cooked under a broiler. Any combination of beef, veal, pork or lamb may be used, in equal parts, as alternatives to the beef and pork given here. Serve the Cevapcici in the traditional fashion, if you choose: with chopped onion, hot peppers, fresh bread and the potent plum brandy called Slivovitz.

What's Cooking
Bill Kuretich
Torrance, California

Makes 20 to 25 meat rolls

2 cloves garlic
½ teaspoon soft green peppercorns
1 pound boneless beef, cubed
1 pound boneless pork, cubed
1 teaspoon salt
1 teaspoon marjoram
1 teaspoon paprika
2 tablespoons chicken or beef broth
2 dashes Tabasco sauce
1 egg

Put one clove of garlic and half the peppercorns into the food processor fitted with the steel blade. Process until coarsely chopped. Add half of the beef cubes, half of the pork cubes, and ½ teaspoon each of salt, marjoram and paprika. Add 1 tablespoon of broth and a dash or two of Tabasco. Process until the meat is chopped to hamburger consistency. Remove to a large clean bowl and repeat the process using all the remaining ingredients except the egg. Combine both batches in the large bowl. Add the egg and mix well. Cover and chill for 1 hour.

Form the meat into sausage shapes about 3 inches long and about ¾ inch in diameter, handling as little as possible, and pressing the meat together only as much as necessary to hold its shape.

Place the meat rolls side by side in a broiler pan. Cook slowly under medium-hot broiler heat until well browned, turning often.

South Seas Dip

This dip is particularly attractive when served in a hollowed pineapple half and surrounded by raw vegetables arranged in color-contrast groupings – such as zucchini and carrot sticks, cauliflower and broccoli florets, mushrooms and cherry tomatoes — and chunks of fresh pineapple. The dip is best prepared a day ahead to allow the ingredients to blend in flavor.

Potluck
Walter O. Angel
Fredericksburg, Virginia

Makes 2 cups

½ cup plain yogurt
½ cup mayonnaise
4 ounces cream cheese
2 tablespoons chopped fresh chives
1 small can water chestnuts,
    drained and finely chopped
6 tablespoons finely chopped candied ginger,
    soaked in water to remove sugar
1½ teaspoons soy sauce
1-2 cloves garlic, finely chopped

   Blend the yogurt, mayonnaise and cream cheese together in a blender or food processor, then combine with all the other ingredients in a bowl; refrigerate, preferably overnight.

Brie and Leek Quiche
(Flamiches au Brie de Meaux)

Gilda Latzky
New York, New York

Makes 1 9-inch quiche
Preheat oven to 350 degrees

9 tablespoons unsalted butter
1 cup julienne-sliced leeks
9-inch quiche crust, partially cooked
½ pound overripe Brie cheese, cut in bits
6 slices bacon, crisply fried,
    drained and crumbled
6 egg yolks
2 cups heavy cream
Salt
Pinch of cayenne pepper

   Heat the butter in a frying pan and sauté the leeks for about 10 minutes. In the quiche shell spread first the leeks, then the cheese and crumbled bacon.
   Beat together the egg yolks and cream with a wire whisk. Add the salt and cayenne pepper, and pour the mixture over the leeks, cheese and bacon.
   Bake in preheated oven for 30 minutes, or until a knife inserted in the center comes out clean; the surface should be well browned. Serve hot.

Cold Artichokes with Basil Dip

This recipe can be a godsend for a busy hostess: both the artichokes and the dip may be prepared ahead of time and refrigerated until ready for use. The dip, in fact, will keep well in the refrigerator for weeks, and is excellent as well with pasta or crudités.

Hilltop Herb Farm
Gwen Barclay and Madalene Hill
Cleveland, Texas

Serves 4

4 artichokes
4 cloves garlic
2 tablespoons vegetable oil
2 teaspoons whole coriander seeds
1 tablespoon salt

DIP:
1 cup lime or lemon juice
⅓ cup fresh basil leaves
2 large cloves garlic
⅓ cup parsley
1 teaspoon salt
2 cups mayonnaise, preferably homemade

Wash the artichokes carefully. Trim the top from each one, remove all the points of the leaves, and cut off the stems. Place the artichokes in a deep pan and cover with water. Add the garlic, oil, coriander seeds and salt. Cover and cook for 35 to 40 minutes until a leaf can be pulled away easily. Spoon the cooking liquid over the artichokes occasionally to distribute the coriander and garlic evenly. Let them cool in the cooking water.

When cool enough to handle, remove from the water and turn them upside down to drain. Shake off any concentration of coriander seeds and garlic. Transfer them, still upside down, to a towel-covered plate and refrigerate.

Prepare the dip: Combine the lime or lemon juice, basil, garlic, parsley and salt in a blender or food processor and blend until smooth. Combine the mixture with the mayonnaise and taste for seasoning. Add more salt if needed. Chill until serving time.

When ready to serve, remove the choke from each artichoke. Spread the leaves and reach down with the fingertips to the firm base of the heart. Rubbing gently where the choke meets the heart, roll the choke into a ball to remove. Be sure to get the last bit of choke out. This will give you a neat cavity for the dipping sauce.

Just before serving, spoon or pour the dipping sauce into the artichokes, being careful not to drip on the leaves.

Salmon Mousse

This may be made ahead and frozen for several weeks until needed.

Charcuterie Cooking School of Food and Wine
Scottie McKinney
San Francisco, California

Serves 6 to 8

2 envelopes unflavored gelatin
3 tablespoons lemon juice
2 tablespoons grated onion
2 tablespoons chopped capers
1 tablespoon dill weed
¼ teaspoon paprika
½ teaspooon Tabasco sauce
1 teaspoon salt
3 cups cooked salmon
1½ cups sour cream
1 cup heavy cream, whipped

   Pour the gelatin into ½ cup of water and heat it until it dissolves. Add all the remaining ingredients except the whipped cream, and puree in a blender or food processor. Fold in the whipped cream. Turn into an oiled mold or springform pan. Chill for several hours or overnight. Unmold and serve with thin slices of French bread.

Picante Shrimp

Use more or less of the jalapeños for this recipe, depending on your taste for hot food.

The Lemon Tree
Charlotte Kuppinger
Harlingen, Texas

Makes 2 to 2½ quarts

2 pounds shrimp, briefly boiled, then peeled
2 lemons, thinly sliced
1 onion, thinly sliced
½ cup chopped pimiento
½ cup pitted ripe olives, sliced
½ cup vegetable oil
¼ to ½ cup chopped jalapeños
2 tablespoons wine vinegar
1 cup lemon juice
1 clove garlic, crushed
1½ teaspoons salt
1 teaspoon freshly ground pepper
¼ teaspoon cayenne pepper
¼ teaspoon dry mustard
1 bay leaf, broken

   Mix together the shrimp, lemon slices, onion, pimiento and olives. Stir all the remaining ingredients together and pour over the shrimp mixture. Chill for 24 hours or up to one week, stirring occasionally. Serve chilled.

Shrimp Toast

The Chinese icicle radish in this recipe is also known as Chinese turnip or Japanese dicon. The Mexican radish called Jicima can be used instead, or fresh water chestnuts can be substituted as a last resort if neither of the others is available.

Karen Lee's Chinese Cooking Classes
Karen Lee
New York, New York

Serves 6

½ pound shrimp, shelled, washed,
   dried and minced
½ tablespoon dark soy sauce
1 teaspoon sherry
1 tablespoon water chestnut powder
¼ cup Chinese icicle radish, minced
2 teaspoons fresh ginger root, minced
2 scallions, including green parts, chopped
½ teaspoon salt
¼ teaspoon freshly ground white pepper
½ teaspoon sugar
6 slices white bread, preferably a bit stale
⅓ cup sesame seeds (optional)
4 cups peanut oil for deep frying

Put the shrimp in a bowl.
Combine the soy sauce and sherry and dissolve the water chestnut powder in the mixture. Add to the minced shrimp, along with the icicle radish, ginger, scallions, salt, pepper and sugar. Using a whisk or, preferably, holding several chopsticks in one hand, stir the shrimp mixture until it is well combined. Refrigerate for 1 to 24 hours. If the bread is fresh, lay the slices separately on a flat surface and leave them for 2 hours to dry out; then turn them over and leave for another 2 hours.

(Fresh bread will absorb too much of the oil).
Spread the shrimp mixture on the 6 pieces of bread, using an icing spatula. Sprinkle with sesame seeds (if used). Cut each slice into 4 triangles. They may be refrigerated at this point for up to 3 hours, or fried at once. If refrigerating, remove them half an hour before frying, to come to room temperature.
Place a 14-inch wok over high heat for about a minute. Pour in the 4 cups of oil, reduce the heat to medium and wait until a thermometer registers 350 degrees. Turn the heat again to high. Holding one triangle in your fingers, gently lower the bread into the oil, shrimp side down. Add eleven more, and fry all 24 in two batches, turning each triangle over after about a minute, to fry for a minute longer, or until the toast has turned brown. Remove with a flat wire strainer or a slotted spatula and let drain on several layers of paper towel. Serve immediately.

Mushrooms with Spinach-Cheese Filling, Microwave
(Gomo de Espinaca)

This is a deliciously low-calorie appetizer. It should be eaten while the mushrooms are still quite firm. Although the spinach filling may be prepared in advance, it should not be put into the mushroom caps until the last minute.

Microwave Cooking Center, Inc.
Thelma Pressman
Encino, California

Makes 24 appetizers

10-ounce package frozen spinach
½ cup grated Parmesan cheese
4 ounces feta cheese, crumbled
½ cup finely chopped scallions
½ cup finely chopped parsley
Salt
24 medium-size mushrooms, cleaned and with stems removed

Place the package of spinach in the microwave oven and cook 3 minutes to defrost. Remove the spinach from the package and drain well in a colander, pressing out the moisture gently with a wooden spoon.

Transfer to a mixing bowl and add the cheeses, scallions, parsley and salt to taste. Mix well. This can now be saved in a cool place, until almost ready to serve.

Fill the mushroom caps with the mixture and place them on a serving plate, cook them in the microwave oven 3 to 4 minutes and serve steaming hot.

Dijon Ham Spread

Serve on crackers or rounds of rye.

Barbara C. Heiken
Cincinnati, Ohio

Makes 1½ cups

1 cup ham, cut into 1-inch cubes
1 large sweet pickle, cubed
½ cup grated Swiss cheese
¼ cup finely chopped parsley
3 tablespoons Dijon mustard
½ cup mayonnaise
10 drops Tabasco sauce

Put the ham and pickle cubes into the food processor fitted with the steel blade. Process for a few seconds. Add the Swiss cheese, parsley, mustard, mayonnaise and Tabasco, and process for about 10 seconds. The texture should be fairly coarse.

Cucumber Caraway Tart

Modern Gourmet of Milwaukee
Myra Dorros
Milwaukee, Wisconsin

Serves 8 to 10
Preheat oven to 400 degrees

Pie crust dough for a 9- or 10-inch pie
2 tablespoons unsalted butter
1 large cucumber, peeled and sliced
Salt
Pepper
3 egg yolks
1½ cups heavy cream
1½ tablespoons caraway seeds
5 slices caraway brick cheese

Bake the pie crust blind, for 15 to 20 minutes in the preheated oven. Remove, and reduce oven heat to 350 degrees.

Meanwhile, heat the butter in a frying pan and sauté the cucumber slices until just softened. Add salt and pepper to taste. Drain the cucumber slices and place in the pie shell. Mix the egg yolks and cream together. Add the caraway seeds and a little more salt and pepper. Pour the mixture over the cucumbers and cover with the cheese.

Bake in the preheated oven at 350 degrees for 40 minutes or until the custard has thickened and the top is golden brown. Let the tart cool for 10 minutes before serving.

First Courses

Q: *What is a first course?* **A:** *A dish served at the table to get the meal off to a good start. First courses should be light; they may be tantalizing — teasing to the palate, some cooks say — but they must never be satiating. Like hors d'oeuvres, they coax the tastebuds into alert readiness for the delicious foods to come.*

The English tradition, from which many of us derive our customs in dining sequence, solidly favored fish or seafood as a first course. This was usually preceded by the soup, whereas we tend — at least in this book — to put a little solid food first. Either way, along with many of the Europeans, we are as likely to crave something fresh from the garden as something fresh from the sea.

American dishes tend to predominate in this section, but you will find as well various international items —a spicy Indian dish of mussels, an Italian omelette, a French soufflé, an Italian pasta with salmon, and several Chinese dishes, both imaginative and classic. All are distinguished by intriguing blends of texture and flavor, the better to lead you on.

Shrimp with Garlic, Oil and Herbs

These shrimp are picked up in the fingers and peeled as they are eaten; such a delightfully messy first course will break the ice at the stuffiest gathering. Serve them with crusty bread that can be dipped into the hot flavored oil — and finger bowls or hot moist napkins.

Irena Chalmers
New York, New York

Serves 4
Preheat the broiler

1½ pounds large shrimp (about 32), shells on
Kosher or coarse sea salt
¾ cup olive oil
4-6 large cloves garlic, peeled
¼ cup parsley
4 lemon wedges

Roll the shrimp in the salt and put them into 4 shallow baking dishes.

Put the oil, garlic and parsley in the food processor with the steel blade; process until finely chopped. Pour the mixture over the shrimp.

Broil on the bottom shelf of the broiler for 5 minutes until the shells are bright pink and the shrimp opaque. Garnish with lemon wedges.

Lamb in Aspic

Mary Beth Clark
New York, New York

Serves 4

1 pound lamb from the leg, trimmed and cut into 2-inch pieces
½-inch slice of fresh ginger, peeled
2 cloves garlic
2 scallions, cut in half
1 star anise
1 teaspoon grated tangerine peel
2 cups beef broth combined with 2 cups water
3 tablespoons light soy sauce
2 tablespoons shao-hsing wine or dry sherry
1 teaspoon granulated sugar
1 tablespoon gelatin dissolved in ⅓ cup water

Place the lamb in a saucepan and cover with water. Bring to a boil and cook for 3 minutes. Drain and discard the water. Place all the ingredients except the gelatin in the saucepan and bring to a boil. Lower heat and simmer for 1½ to 2 hours, or until the lamb is very tender.

Remove the lamb and cool. Strain the liquid. There should be 1 cup of liquid; if not, add enough water to make 1 cup. Pour the liquid into a saucepan and add the gelatin. Heat and stir until the gelatin has dissolved and a clear liquid has formed.

Cut the lamb into slices ¼ inch thick. Arrange the slices in a small mold and add the liquid. Refrigerate for at least 4 hours. To serve, unmold and slice thickly. Arrange the aspic slices overlapping one another on a serving platter.

Oysters and Escargots

As a first course, these should be served with three oysters and three snails on each serving plate, masked in sauce. The recipe can also easily be doubled and served from a chafing-dish at a cocktail party, in which case it is wise to prepare considerably more than you anticipate you should need. Be cautious not to overcook.

Seasonal Kitchen
Jean Sparks
Huntsville, Alabama

Serves 8

SAUCE:
1 tablespoon butter
1 large clove garlic, minced
2 teaspoons anchovy paste
Grated peel of 1 lemon
Grated peel of 1 orange
2 cups heavy cream
Salt
Freshly ground black pepper

7½-ounce can imported snails (2 dozen)
1 small onion, minced
1 bay leaf, crumbled
2 dozen fresh oysters

To make the sauce, heat the butter and sauté the garlic for 2 minutes. Add the anchovy paste and lemon and orange rinds; cook for 2 minutes over low heat. Add the cream, turn up the heat and cook, stirring, until the mixture reduces to about 1 cup, being careful not to scorch. Add salt and pepper to taste.

Put the snails and the liquid from the can into a saucepan. Add the onion and bay leaf and simmer 10 minutes. Let it cool. Drain off the liquid and pat the snails dry with paper towels.

Poach the oysters in simmering water for 1 minute only. Drain and pat dry with paper towels. Heat the oysters and snails in the hot sauce and serve at once.

Tomato Vegetable Pâté

This is an ideal first course for summertime dining al fresco, served on a bed of fresh spinach leaves, with homemade mayonnaise. It can also be served with crackers as an hors d'oeuvre for standup eating, or with crusty bread for a light luncheon.

Kitchen Bazaar
Barbara Smith Jeffress
Washington, D.C.

Serves 8 to 10

1 large can plum tomatoes packed in puree
1 cucumber, peeled, seeded and chopped
1 small red onion, quartered
2 cloves garlic
3 tablespoons olive oil
2 tablespoons red wine vinegar
3 tablespoons tomato paste
1 teaspoon celery salt
1 teaspoon red pepper flakes
3-4 drops Tabasco sauce
2 green peppers, seeds and membranes
  removed and finely chopped
3 packages unflavored gelatin
½ cup vodka
Oil for greasing pan
1 avocado, sliced
½ can black olives, sliced
¼ pound mushrooms, sliced

Puree the canned tomatoes with their liquid in a food processor fitted with a steel blade and transfer to a large bowl. In the processor combine and finely chop the cucumber, onion, garlic, oil, vinegar, tomato paste, celery salt, pepper flakes, Tabasco and one of the green peppers. Add to the pureed tomato and stir to mix well.

In the top of a double boiler, dissolve the gelatin in the vodka over boiling water. Stir until a clear liquid has formed, then add to the vegetable tomato mixture. Stir well. Chill until on the point of setting.

Oil a large loaf pan and spoon in a layer of the tomato mixture. Add a layer of avocado slices, then another layer of the tomato mixture. On top of that place a layer of olive and mushroom slices, then another of the tomato mixture. Finally add a layer of chopped green pepper and cover with the remaining tomato mixture. Cover with wax paper and chill overnight.

When ready to serve, unmold the pâté by running a knife around the pan edges and inverting it on a tray. Slice carefully before serving.

Spinach in Artichoke Bottoms, Microwave

Alice Copeland Phillips
Atlanta, Georgia

Serves 6 to 8

3 10-ounce packages frozen chopped spinach
8 ounces cream cheese
1 medium-size onion, chopped
½ cup mayonnaise
1 egg
1 teaspoon dill weed
1 teaspoon salt
½ teaspoon pepper
2 cans artichoke bottoms, rinsed in water and
    drained
3 tablespoons grated Parmesan cheese
1 teaspoon paprika

Defrost the spinach by pricking the packages and placing them, all on one plate, in the microwave oven for 6 to 8 minutes at high. Drain thoroughly, pressing out the moisture with a fork.

Soften the cream cheese by removing the foil wrap and microwaving at 50% power ½ minute to 1 minute.

Combine the cream cheese, onion, mayonnaise, egg, dill weed, salt and pepper in a bowl and fold in the spinach. Spoon the mixture into the artichoke bottoms. Sprinkle the top of each mound with Parmesan and paprika. Place them on a plate to microwave in batches of about 6, for 1½ to 3 minutes on 80% power.

Italian Omelette
(Frittata)

This is an Eastertime favorite among Italians.

Virginia Stefani
Pittsburgh, Pennsylvania

Serves 10

4 tablespoons olive oil
1 cup asparagus in ½-inch pieces
¾ cup scallions in ½-inch pieces
¾ cup green pepper in ½-inch squares
12 eggs
⅓ cup milk
⅓ cup grated Parmesan cheese
¾ cup ricotta cheese, diced
¼ cup finely chopped parsley
Salt
Pepper

Heat the oil in a 12-inch skillet and sauté the asparagus, scallions and green pepper until soft.

Meanwhile beat the eggs in a bowl and add the milk and cheeses. Add the parsley, salt and pepper. Pour the mixture over the vegetables in the skillet. Stir lightly and cook over low-to-medium heat. Make sure the bottom does not stick to the pan.

When the bottom and sides are well set, turn the frittata over carefully. First slide it onto a flat plate, then invert the skillet over it and reverse. The uncooked side of the frittata will then be on the bottom of the pan. Cook another 4 minutes, then slide it onto a warmed platter and serve. If necessary, it can be kept warm in a 250-degree oven for a short time. It is also very good served at room temperature.

Escargot Tart

Perla Meyers
New York, New York

Serves 6 to 8
Preheat oven to 350 degrees

TART DOUGH:
2 cups flour
12 tablespoons unsalted butter
Pinch of salt
5 tablespoons ice water

2 cans well drained escargots
2 cups full-bodied chicken broth
1 bouquet garni
4-6 tablespoons butter
2 tablespoons finely minced shallots
2 tablespoons finely minced parsley
3 large garlic cloves, finely minced
1½ cups heavy cream
2 eggs
2 eggs yolks
Salt
Freshly ground white pepper
2 tablespoons freshly grated Parmesan cheese

Combine the flour, butter and salt; mix well. Gradually add the ice water to form a dough. Line a 9- or 10-inch pie dish and bake the crust in the preheated oven just until starting to brown.
Place the drained escargots in a saucepan with the broth and bouquet garni and poach over low heat for 20 minutes. If the escargots are very large they may be cut in half at this point. Drain and reserve. In a small heavy skillet heat the butter. Add the herbs and escargots and toss the mixture in the herb butter over low heat for 2 minutes. Set aside.

Combine the 2 egg yolks with the 2 whole eggs and the cream in a bowl. Season with salt and pepper and whisk until well blended. Add the escargot mixture, stir lightly and spoon into the prebaked tart shell. Sprinkle with grated cheese and bake for 35 minutes, or until nicely browned.

Roulades of Spinach and Beef

These flavorful rolls can be frozen after they are baked, then reheated for 15 minutes in a preheated 350-degree oven.

Felicia Slavik
Mount Prospect, Illinois

Makes 20 small roulades
Preheat oven to 375 degrees

10-ounce package frozen chopped spinach, thawed and drained
½ pound finely ground round steak
½ cup feta cheese
½ cup finely chopped onions
½ teaspoon garlic powder
Generous pinch seasoned pepper
¼ teaspoon seasoned salt
5 strips filo or strudel pastry, 3 inches by 12 inches

Place the drained spinach, ground beef, feta cheese, onion and garlic powder in a blender and blend about 2 minutes until smooth. Cut the dough into 3-inch squares. Place 1 tablespoon of the mixture in the middle of each piece. Roll up, tucking in the sides first. Brush with beaten egg and arrange on a baking sheet. Bake for 25 minutes.

Pasta with Smoked Salmon
(Tagliarini al Salmone)

This is a recipe from the Grand Hotel in Rome. Do not serve cheese with it: Chef Paolo Moretti insists cheese should never be served with fish dishes.

Pampered Pantry
Marie Mosher
St. Louis, Missouri

Serves 4 to 6

4 thin slices smoked salmon
2¼ cups heavy cream
1 tablespoon flour
4 tablespoons soft butter
1 pound linguini noodles
¼ teaspoon white pepper

Cut the salmon into fine julienne strips and set aside.

Heat 2 cups heavy cream in a heavy saucepan. Mix the flour and 1 tablespoon of the butter together in bits, to make a beurre manie. Add to the cream bit by bit over medium heat, stirring continuously with a whisk. When the sauce is smooth and thickened, add the salmon and continue cooking over low heat for several minutes to blend the flavors.

Meanwhile cook the noodles in a generous amount of boiling water until lightly done ("al dente"). Rinse under cold running water very briefly, to stop further cooking. Transfer to a warm serving dish and stir in the remaining 3 tablespoons of butter and ¼ cup of cream. Season with the white pepper and toss with the hot salmon sauce.

Seafood-Stuffed Artichokes

Sally Bernstein
Houston, Texas

Serves 5
Preheat oven to 375 degrees

5 fresh artichokes
1 teaspoon olive oil
3 cloves garlic, peeled
6-ounce package frozen crabmeat,
    thawed and drained
16-ounce package frozen shrimp,
    thawed and drained
1 cup grated Swiss cheese
⅓ cup chopped green pepper
1 teaspoon salt
½ cup mayonnaise
2 teaspoons lemon juice

Place the artichokes in boiling salted water to cover. Add the olive oil and garlic. Cover and simmer 45 minutes to 1 hour, until a leaf can be pulled easily from an artichoke.

Meanwhile, flake the crabmeat and cut the shrimps in half, if using large shrimp. Toss with the cheese, green pepper and salt. Mix the mayonnaise and lemon juice together, and add to the mixture. Stir well.

Remove the small center leaves of each artichoke and carefully remove the choke, leaving a cup shape.

Fill these artichoke cups with the seafood mixture and place the artichokes upright in a baking dish. Pour hot water around them to about 1 inch depth. Cover and bake in the preheated oven 35 minutes or until heated through.

Spareribs in Black Bean Sauce

Catherine Kunkle
New Richmond, Wisconsin

Serves 4 to 6

1½ pounds pork back ribs, cut across the bone
   into 1-inch strips by butcher
2 tablespoons black beans, rinsed and drained
3 cloves garlic, minced
2 slices fresh ginger, each roughly the
   dimensions of a 25-cent piece
¾ cup chicken broth
2 tablespoons dark soy sauce
1 tablespoon dry sherry
1 teaspoon sugar
3 scallions, cleaned and shredded, including
   green parts
1 teaspoon cornstarch
1 teaspoon sesame oil

Cut between the ribs to form 1-inch squares.
Place the wok, dry, over heat. When it is smoking,
add the rib squares in small batches, to brown.
They will render their own fat. As the batches are
browned, transfer them to a casserole in a
warm place.

Mash the black beans, garlic and ginger together
to form a paste. Combine the chicken broth, soy
sauce, sherry and sugar.

When all the ribs have been transferred to the
casserole, pour off all but 1 tablespoon of the fat
from the wok. Add the black bean paste and stir-
fry for half a minute. Add the chicken broth
mixture, stir and simmer 1 minute. Pour the
mixture over the ribs in the casserole, and scatter
the shredded scallions on top. Cover the casserole
and simmer 1 hour, or until tender.

In the wok, dissolve the cornstarch in 3
teaspoons water and cook until thickened. Add the
sesame oil and pour the mixture into the casserole.
Mix well and serve immediately.

Artichoke Hearts and Seafood au Gratin

Susan B. Langhorne
Hilton Head Island, South Carolina

Serves 6 to 10

4 tablespoons butter
4 tablespoons flour
1 cup milk
1 pound cream cheese
1 pound fresh shrimp, peeled, cleaned and
   coarsely chopped
1 pound fresh crabmeat
1 can artichoke hearts,
   drained and coarsely chopped
2 teaspoons Dijon mustard
½ pound Swiss cheese, grated
1 cup white wine
White pepper

Heat the butter in a saucepan. Add the flour and
stir constantly for a minute or two over low heat.
Add the milk gradually and continue stirring until
the mixture thickens. Add the cream cheese, a little
at a time, stirring with a whisk to incorporate it as it
melts. Add the remaining ingredients, stirring as
the mixture cooks over low heat. It can be

transferred to a chafing dish to finish cooking, or can be served in individual gratin dishes over toast points. After the shrimp is added, the entire cooking process should not exceed about 10 minutes, or the shrimp will toughen.

Mushrooms in Parchment
(Funghi 'Ncartati)

This unusual first-course dish will be of particular interest to country-dwelling mushroom gatherers, as the recipe calls for either edible wild or domesticated mushrooms. In either case, choose firm young mushrooms with white, tight caps as freshly picked as possible. The word "'ncartati" is a Sicilian version of "in cartoccio" (which is Italian for "en papillote").

Carlo Middione
San Francisco, California

Serves 4
Preheat oven to 350 degrees

1 pound fresh mushrooms, edible wild or
   commercially produced
8 anchovy fillets, rinsed and finely chopped
4 heaping tablespoons finely chopped parsley,
   preferably the Italian variety
Freshly ground black pepper
2 large cloves garlic, finely chopped
4 tablespoons breadcrumbs
4 tablespoons olive oil
Juice of 1 lemon
4 thin slices lemon for garnish
20-inch square of parchment paper
   or brown paper

Wipe the mushrooms clean. Do not wash them unless really necessary. Cut into thin slices and place in a large bowl. Add all the other ingredients except the lemon slices, and mix well.

Brush the paper square with oil and spoon the mushroom mixture onto the center in a mound. Place the lemon slices on top. Fold up the paper to enclose the mushroom mixture, sealing the edges very well by making many overlapping little folds. Brush the outside of the paper packet all over with oil and place on a baking sheet.

Bake for 15 minutes in the preheated oven. Do not overcook. Tear open the paper and serve piping hot.

Eggplant Mushroom Strudels

These strudels can be prepared ahead and reheated (for 25 minutes at 375 degrees).

The Tasting Spoon
Tucson, Arizona

Serves 8 to 16
Preheat oven to 375 degrees

1 medium-size eggplant (about 1½ pounds), peeled and diced
1 medium-size onion, chopped
1 large clove garlic, finely chopped
½ pound mushrooms, sliced
4 tablespoons butter
1½ cups grated Swiss cheese
½ cup grated Parmesan cheese
¼ cup chopped parsley
2 eggs
½ teaspoon basil
½ teaspoon oregano
1 teaspoon salt
½ cup breadcrumbs
1 pound filo dough, at room temperature
½ cup melted butter
8-ounce carton sour cream

Cook the eggplant in ½ cup water until tender. Drain and set aside. In a large skillet sauté the onion, garlic and mushrooms in the butter until the moisture has evaporated. Stir in the eggplant and mash with a fork. Add the cheeses, eggs, seasonings and breadcrumbs and mix well.

Unwrap the filo dough and spread it out to lie flat. Cover with a damp towel or plastic wrap. Lay one sheet of the filo on a buttered baking sheet. Brush with melted butter, cover with another sheet of filo dough and brush with melted butter. Spoon about ⅔ cup of the filling mixture along one of the short sides of the dough, 2 inches from the edges. Fold the dough over the ends of the line of filling and roll up loosely. Repeat to make 8 rolls. Brush all the rolls with melted butter. Score each roll at 1-inch intervals, and bake in the preheated oven 35 minutes until golden brown.

Cut in 1-inch slices and serve with sour cream.

Marinated Antipasto
(Antipasto Marinata)

Serve this appetizer arrayed on a platter, with plenty of warm crusty French bread.

Complete Cuisine
Alexandra (Sandi) Cooper
Ann Arbor, Michigan

Serves 8 to 10

1 cup olive oil
Juice of 2 lemons
1 tablespoon tomato paste
Freshly ground pepper
½ teaspoon rosemary, crushed
1 pound shrimp, cleaned and cooked
1 can oil-packed tuna, drained and flaked
2 jars (6 ounces each) marinated artichokes
8-ounce can sardines, drained
1 can flat anchovies, drained and rinsed
2-ounce jar pimientos, drained
½ can pitted black olives, drained
6 ounces fresh mushrooms, cleaned and sliced
2 dill (preferably not kosher dill) pickles, sliced

Combine the oil, lemon juice, tomato paste, pepper and rosemary. Arrange all the remaining ingredients in layers in a deep bowl. Cover with the oil mixture and refrigerate at least 4 hours.

Soufflé La Varenne

This soufflé is based on duxelles mushroom puree and named for François Pierre, Sieur de la Varenne, who was chef to the Marquis d'Uxelles in the mid-seventeenth century. Nevertheless, it is typical of today's very modern nouvelle cuisine since the soufflé contains no flour.

École de Cuisine La Varenne
Anne Willan and Gregory Usher
Paris, France

Serves 4
Preheat oven to 400 degrees

2 tablespoons butter
½ onion, very finely chopped
½ pound mushrooms, very finely chopped
Squeeze of lemon juice
1 tablespoon chopped parsely
Pinch of nutmeg
Salt
Pepper
¾ cup heavy cream
4 egg yolks
6 egg whites

Heat the butter in a sauté pan and cook the onion until soft but not browned. Add the mushrooms and lemon juice and cook over high heat, stirring occasionally, until the mixture is dry and all the moisture has evaporated. Stir in the parsley, nutmeg, salt and pepper. Remove from heat and stir in the cream.

Add the 4 egg yolks to the puree and return to the heat. Cook, stirring constantly, just until the puree thickens slightly, showing that the yolks are cooked. Remove from the heat at once or it will curdle. Taste, adjust the seasoning and let cool.

At this stage the mixture can be refrigerated for 6 to 8 hours if desired. The surface should first be rubbed with a piece of butter to prevent a skin forming.

Butter a 1-quart soufflé dish and place in the refrigerator to chill until it is needed.

Heat the mushroom mixture over low heat until hot to the touch. Meanwhile, beat the 6 egg whites until stiff. Stir one quarter of the egg whites into the mushroom mixture. The heat of the mushrooms will cook the egg whites and lighten the mixture. Add the mushroom mixture to the remaining egg whites, folding together as lightly as possible. Spoon the mixture into the cold soufflé dish and bake in the preheated oven for 15 to 20 minutes until the soufflé is puffed and brown. Serve immediately.

Tomato Mousse Nests
(Les Petits Nids)

This recipe is for the mousse that is served so exquisitely at Taillevent in Paris. It is piped through a pastry bag to form nest shapes, which are then filled with a variety of delicacies. If you prefer, the mousse can be served far less elaborately, simply spooned into a mound on a bed of lettuce, and it will still be delicious. If you fill the mousse with quail eggs, allow three per serving; if caviar, one teaspoon each.

Diane Wilkinson
Atlanta, Georgia

Serves 6 to 8
Preheat oven to 350 degrees

4 tablespoons butter
1½ cups chopped carrots
1½ cups chopped onions
¼ cup chopped shallots
½ cup chopped leeks
5 large tomatoes, coarsely chopped,
   skins and seeds removed
1 teaspoon salt
White pepper
1 bay leaf
1 sprig of parsley
¼ teaspoon thyme
Small bunch of celery leaves
1 package gelatin
2 tablespoons tomato juice
¾ cup heavy cream
Salt
Pepper
For garnish: slivered lettuce
   and to fill the "nests": poached
   quail eggs, fresh cooked asparagus tips,
   fresh peas or black caviar

Melt the butter in an ovenproof saucepan and toss the carrots, onions, shallots and leeks over low heat. Cook gently 15 minutes, stirring occasionally so the vegetables do not brown. Add the tomatoes, salt, pepper, bay leaf, parsley, thyme and celery leaves. Mix well. Put the pan in the preheated oven and cook about 2 hours, checking occasionally and stirring. Remove from the oven when all the excess liquid has evaporated.

Pass the tomato sauce through a food mill, tami or sieve to extract all the tender pulp. This pureed base for the mousse can be refrigerated overnight, or even frozen, at this stage.

Place the puree in a saucepan and reheat it gently. Dissolve the gelatin in the tomato juice and add. Stir over low heat for 1 minute. Remove from the heat and cool to room temperature. Beat the cream until thickened and stir it into the cool puree. Season to taste with salt and pepper. To shape, the mousse should be slightly softer than an uncooked meringue; refrigerate for an hour or two if necessary to obtain the correct consistency.

Spoon the puree into a pastry bag with a medium-large star tip. Pipe a circular 3-inch nest shape on a bed of slivered lettuce. Form the sides 2 inches high. Fill the nest with poached quail eggs, lightly cooked asparagus tips, fresh peas or black caviar.

Pasta with Zucchini and Walnuts

This recipe offers alternative methods of making the pasta, the first using a food processor and pasta machine, the other by hand. As a third alternative, dried pasta (12 ounces to 1 pound) may be used, but fresh homemade pasta is always best. This is tossed in a cream sauce and mixed with zucchini and walnuts just before serving. The cream sauce may be prepared ahead of time and kept in the refrigerator. The zucchini-walnut mixture can be prepared a few hours in advance. Both will need brief reheating at the last minute.

Sara E. Sharpe
Miami, Florida

Serves 6
Preheat oven to 400 degrees

1¼-1¾ cups unbleached flour
2 large eggs
¼ teaspoon salt

SAUCE:
2 cups heavy cream
½ cup freshly grated Parmesan cheese
Pinch of nutmeg
Salt
Pepper
4 tablespoons butter
1½ cups zucchini cut in 1½-inch julienne strips

1 cup shelled walnuts

Put 1¼ cups flour in a food processor bowl with knife blade. Add the eggs and salt and process until a ball of dough is formed. Then count 60 revolutions of the ball before switching off. Roll out and cut the pasta into fettucine with a pasta machine, adding flour as necessary to achieve a smooth, satiny texture.

To make the pasta by hand, put 1¼ cups flour on the board and make a well in the center. Add the eggs and salt. With a fork, mix together until a fairly stiff dough is formed. Knead vigorously for 4 to 5 minutes or until the dough is smooth and satiny. Let it rest for 20 minutes, then roll out with a rolling pin to a thickness of 1/16 inch or less. Cut noodles about ¼ inch wide.

To make the sauce, boil the cream until it is thick, reducing it to about 1½ cups. Stir in the Parmesan cheese and add nutmeg, salt and pepper to taste. Remove from heat and keep warm.

Meanwhile, set a large quantity of salted water to boil.

Put the butter in a skillet and sauté the zucchini very briefly, only long enough to remove the raw taste. Remove from the skillet to a warm bowl and toss the walnuts in the butter remaining in the skillet. Add to the zucchini, and salt the mixture lightly.

Boil the pasta in the salted water just until cooked. Fresh pasta will need only 2 to 3 minutes. Drain well and toss with the cream sauce. Stir in the zucchini mixture and serve at once.

Quenelles with Shrimp Sauce
(Quenelles Velouté aux Crevettes)

These quenelles are composed of cream puff pastry combined with pureed raw fish.

Joanne Donsky
San Francisco, California

Makes 16 to 24 quenelles
Preheat oven to 400 degrees

1 cup butter, chilled
½ cup milk
½ cup flour
¾ teaspoon salt
¼ teaspoon white pepper
3 eggs
2 egg yolks
½ pound boneless raw salmon or halibut
   (about 14 ounces before skinning and boning),
   pureed
1 tablespoon heavy cream

SAUCE:
4 tablespoons butter
4 tablespoons flour
1½ cups fish stock
½ cup heavy cream
Pinch of cayenne pepper
Salt
White pepper
½ cup baby shrimp, slightly cooked
Lemon juice (optional)
4-8 tablespoons butter, softened (optional)

First make the pâte à choux (cream puff pastry): Put 4 tablespoons of the butter, cut in pieces, in a small, heavy saucepan with the milk, and bring to a boil. When the butter is completely melted, remove the pan from the heat and mix in the flour, ½ teaspoon salt and half the pepper, added all at once. Still off the heat, quickly stir the mixture with a wooden spoon, then return the pan to the stove. Beat the mixture vigorously over moderate heat for a couple of minutes until it becomes a thick mass that comes away from the sides of the pan. Remove from the heat. Make a well in the center, break in an egg, and beat quickly. Keep beating until the egg is fully incorporated and the mixture has come together in a solid mass. Add each of the other 2 eggs in the same manner, and then the 2 egg yolks. After the last egg yolk has been added, the mixture should be smooth and shiny, and should fall lazily from a lifted spoon.

Combine the pâte à choux with the pureed fish, the cream and the remaining salt and pepper. Beat, blend or process, adding the remaining cold butter a little at a time, to form a fluffy mixture. Chill until very firm, overnight or for at least 2 hours.

Prepare the velouté sauce: Melt the butter in a 1-quart saucepan. Remove from the heat and stir in the flour. Cook over medium-low heat, stirring, for 1 to 2 minutes. Remove from the heat and add the fish stock, stirring. Return to the heat and add the cayenne, salt and pepper. Bring to boiling point, stirring constantly. As soon as it boils, remove from the heat and add the cream and shrimp. Reheat gently (do not let it boil), taste and add a little lemon juice if needed.

Bring about 4 inches of salted water to the simmering point in a large saucepan. Dip two soup spoons into the hot water to moisten them and, with one of them, scoop out a spoonful of the fish mixture. With the other spoon, round the top over, to form the traditional quenelle shape. Using both spoons, quickly loosen the quenelle and slide it into the simmering water. Repeat the process with the rest of the mixture. Be sure the water is barely simmering, not boiling. Poach the quenelles 12 to

15 minutes, until they turn over easily with a nudge. Remove with a slotted spoon and place in a baking dish. Spoon the velouté sauce over the quenelles, masking them completely, and bake for 15 minutes in the preheated oven. Serve at once.

Spaghetti with Oil, Garlic and Ginger
(Spaghetti Aglio e Olio)

Beverly Cox
Southport, Connecticut

Makes 4 servings

1 tablespoon salt
8 ounces dry spaghetti
3 tablespoons olive oil
2 teaspoons minced fresh ginger
2 teaspoons minced fresh garlic
2 tablespoons minced parsley

Bring 4 quarts of water to a rolling boil and stir in the 1 tablespoon of salt. Add the spaghetti and stir. After 6 minutes, add 1 tablespoon of olive oil to the cooking water and continue cooking for approximately 2 minutes more, or until the spaghetti is just tender.

Meanwhile heat the remaining 2 tablespoons of olive oil to just below a boil. Stir in the ginger, garlic and parsley and remove from heat.

Drain the spaghetti and toss with the sauce. Serve at once.

Gram's Chopped Eggplant

Serve this as an appetizer in a mound on lettuce leaves, with finely sliced onions and fresh ripe tomatoes. Your vegetarian friends will thank you.

Elaine B. Forman
Potomac, Maryland

Serves 4 to 6
Preheat the broiler

1 large eggplant
1 large green pepper
2 tablespoons white vinegar
1 teaspoon vegetable oil
¾ cup fine breadcrumbs
Salt
Freshly ground pepper

Pierce the eggplant in several places. Place the whole eggplant and the green pepper on a piece of foil on the broiler rack and broil, 6 inches from the heat, turning frequently, until the skin is soft and charred.

Remove from the broiler and place the green pepper to cool in a closed plastic bag or wrapped in plastic film. Peel the eggplant as soon as it is cool enough to handle, and place in a wooden chopping bowl or a food processor. Peel the green pepper and discard the seeds and membrane; add to the chopping bowl or food processor. Add the vinegar, oil and breadcrumbs, and chop all the ingredients together, seasoning to taste. If you are using a food processor, be careful not to chop it too finely; it will taste better with the eggplant left a little chunky.

Country Terrine – Low Fat Style

This switch on the usual terrine uses spinach instead of pork fat, adding new interest to the taste and giving it a lovely color. Cornichon pickles are small gherkins. Red bell peppers can be bought packed in vinegar, which should be drained off.

Barbara R. Pisik
Deerfield, Illinois

Serves 8 to 16
Preheat oven to 350 degrees
Grease a 9-by-5-inch loaf pan, or spray it with
   calorie-free non-stick spray.

1½ cups chopped fresh raw spinach, or
   10-ounce package frozen chopped spinach,
   thawed, drained thoroughly and rechopped
½ cup finely chopped onion
1 pound lean ground beef
½ cup whole wheat breadcrumbs
1 teaspoon lemon juice
¾ teaspoon salt
½ teaspoon nutmeg
¼ teaspoon dried basil
⅛ teaspoon pepper
1 tablespoon Dijon mustard
½ cup sliced celery
½ cup chopped parsley
¼ cup skimmed milk
1 clove garlic
2 eggs
Cornichon pickles and sweet red bell peppers
   for garnish

Combine the spinach, onion, beef, breadcrumbs, lemon juice, salt, nutmeg, basil, pepper and half the mustard in a bowl. Put the celery, parsley, milk, garlic and eggs in a food processor and process until the celery is coarsely chopped. Stir into the spinach mixture, handling as little as possible.

Spread half of the mixture in the bottom of the loaf pan. Arrange some of the pickles and peppers in a pretty pattern on the meat and spread the remaining meat on top.

Bake in the preheated oven 1¼ to 1½ hours.

Pour off fat, and let the terrine stand for 20 minutes. Turn it out of the pan carefully, clean the pan and return the terrine to the pan.

Cut a heavy piece of cardboard to fit inside the pan. Wrap the cardboard in foil and place on top of the terrine. Place an even weight (2 unopened cans of tuna will do) on top of the cardboard and refrigerate overnight.

Serve the terrine sliced and decorated with more Cornichons, red bell peppers and Dijon mustard.

Soups

A splendid soup is more than something good to eat. In many cultures, a nice hot bowl of soup is also a standard remedy, effective in the cure of any child or adult suffering from cranky, contrary, or hurt feelings.

Soup conveys caring, and most soups please. Same-day soups are fine, of course, but next-day soups can be even better. Rewarmed the day after they're made, they take on a richer, deeper flavor. Most soups will freeze well, too, so you can always make more than plenty, and put some aside for later.

For a rich soup with a contrast in fresh color and texture, cook some of the ingredients for a long time, until the basic mixture is thick; then, just before serving time, add some fresh raw vegetables and cook them until they are hot through and just tender. You can also achieve contrasts in texture by pureeing some ingredients and leaving others whole.

Soups can serve as dinner-starters, they can constitute an entire lunch or dinner, and are indispensable for late-night comfort on cold winter nights. A steaming bowl of soup accompanied by a salad and some bread of good character will make a wonderful and filling meal at any time.

Best Western Chowder

A crisp green salad and garlic bread go well with this chowder.

Magnolia Kitchen Shoppe
Seattle, Washington

Serves 8

2 cans (8 ounces each) chopped clams
2 bottles (8 ounces each) clam juice
1 large potato, diced
5 slices bacon, diced
1 small onion, finely chopped
½ pound uncooked medium-size shrimp
10-ounce jar medium-size Pacific oysters
8 tablespoons butter
½ teaspoon salt
¼ teaspoon pepper
2 cups milk

Drain the liquid from the chopped clams into a large kettle. Add the bottled clam juice and bring to a boil. Add the potato and simmer, covered, for 10 minutes until tender.

Meanwhile, fry the bacon until crisp. Drain the bacon and discard all but about 1 tablespoon of the bacon fat. Add the onion to the frying pan and sauté until limp and slightly golden, about 5 minutes.

Add the shrimp to the kettle with the potato mixture and simmer just until the shrimp turns pink. With a slotted spoon transfer the onion to the kettle, and stir in the bacon, clams and oysters. Add the butter, salt and pepper and stir until the butter melts, then add the milk. Stir gently until the soup is very hot, but do not let it boil. Serve at once.

Chicken Cucumber Soup

Judith Bell
Chicago, Illinois

Serves 4 to 6

2 small or 1 large cucumber
1 chicken breast, boned and skinned
4 cups rich chicken broth
3 tablespoons sherry
¼ cup scallions cut finely on the bias,
    or 2 tablespoons chopped chives

Wash and peel the cucumber. Cut lengthwise and remove the seeds. Cut into matchstick pieces.

Cut the chicken breast into small pieces.

Bring the broth to a boil, and add the chicken. Cook 3 to 5 minutes. Add the cucumber and cook until just tender. Add the sherry.

Remove from heat and sprinkle with the scallions or chives before serving.

Autumn Soup

(Zuppa d'Autunno)

This soup is served in the Valle d'Aosta in Italy, as an aprés-ski warmer-up.

Mario Cardullo
Washington, D.C.

Serves 6

2 tablespoons unsalted butter
2 small onions, thinly sliced
1 clove garlic, crushed
¾ pound lean bacon, finely chopped
2 pounds canned pumpkin
Salt
Freshly ground black pepper
Pinch of freshly ground nutmeg
1 cup Italian rice
1 pound Fontina cheese, cut into small dice

Heat the butter in a skillet over medium heat. Add onions, garlic, bacon, and sauté until the bacon is rendered and the onion is golden. Remove from heat and discard the garlic clove.

Put the pumpkin in a large pot with 1 quart water. Season with salt, pepper, nutmeg, and bring to a boil. Add the rice and reduce heat. Let simmer for about 20 minutes. Add the bacon mixture and the diced Fontina cheese and cook about 2 minutes more, stirring constantly. Remove from heat and serve in warm bowls topped with a sprinkling of freshly ground black pepper.

Curried Jerusalem Artichoke Soup

Madelaine D. Bullwinkel
Hinsdale, Illinois

Serves 4 to 6

1 pound Jerusalem artichokes
2 tablespoons butter
1 medium-size onion, finely chopped
1 clove garlic, finely chopped
1 teaspoon curry powder
4 cups chicken broth
Juice of ½ lemon
Salt
⅛ teaspoon cayenne pepper

Wash and steam the Jerusalem artichokes in a covered pan for 10 to 15 minutes, or until just cooked through.

Heat the butter and sauté the onion and garlic until slightly colored and soft, about 5 minutes. Set aside.

Cool the cooked Jerusalem artichokes under running water. Slip off the skins and coarsely chop the artichokes.

Put the onion mixture over medium-high heat, add the curry powder and cook, stirring, for about half a minute. Add the Jerusalem artichokes and stir rapidly to coat them thoroughly with the curry.

Add the broth gradually, and bring to a boil. Simmer the soup slowly for 15 minutes. Puree or sieve the soup and put in a clean saucepan.

When almost ready to serve, reheat the soup and add lemon juice and salt to taste. Season each serving with a pinch of cayenne pepper.

Boris' Borscht

One of the world's most fascinating and colorful restaurateurs, Boris Lissanevitch, who escaped from the Bolsheviks in the '20s, danced with the Ballet Russe, lived all over the world, and settled in Nepal 28 years ago, serves this splendid Russian dish at his Yak and Yeti Restaurant in Katmandu, often along with quail eggs and smoked becti flown in from the Bay of Bengal.

Gloria Olson
Nashville, Tennessee

Serves 8

2 pounds beef for soup, including bones
1 large chopped onion
4 tablespoons butter
2 cups shredded cabbage
2 large potatoes, peeled and sliced
2 large carrots, peeled and thickly sliced
2 stalks celery, sliced
1 pound canned tomatoes
1 pound canned sliced beets
Salt
Pepper
1 cup sour cream
1 tablespoon chopped dill weed

Simmer the meat and bones in 2 quarts water in a heavy covered pot for 2 hours. Sauté the onion in the butter and add to the pot with the cabbage, potatoes, carrots, celery and the tomatoes with their juices. Simmer about 1 hour. Then add the beets with their juice, salt and pepper. Simmer about 15 minutes and serve. Top with sour cream and a sprinkling of dill.

French Onion Soup

Creative Cookery, Ltd.
LaVonne S. Tollerud
Honolulu, Hawaii

Serves 8

8 tablespoons butter
4 pounds yellow onions, cut in half lengthwise and sliced very thin
1 tablespoon sugar (optional)
¼ cup flour
2 quarts beef broth
1 cup dry white wine or dry vermouth
2 teaspoons salt
Freshly ground black pepper
8 French bread rounds, toasted
2 cloves garlic, cut across
2 tablespoons melted butter
1 tablespoon brandy
1 cup grated Swiss or Gruyere cheese

Heat the butter in a heavy saucepan. Add the onions and sauté until well cooked and golden brown. Sprinkle with sugar to help brown the onions if they are not as rich in color as you would like. Add the flour and mix well. Add the broth, wine, salt and pepper. Simmer for an hour, uncovered, over low heat.

Rub the toasted bread with the garlic and brush with butter. Put the tablespoon of brandy in the bottom of a shallow soup tureen, ladle in the soup and top with the bread rounds. Sprinkle generously with the grated cheese. Place in a very hot oven or under the broiler until the top is bubbly and brown. Serve at once.

Puree of Carrot Soup

This elegant soup is easy to prepare and low in calories.

Look & Cook
Bunny Dell
Teaneck, New Jersey

Serves 6 to 8

2 tablespoons butter
1 tablespoon oil
2 medium-size onions
1 pound carrots, peeled and thinly sliced
4 cups chicken broth
Salt
Pepper
3 tablespoons finely chopped parsley,
   or 1 cup croutons, for garnish

Heat the butter and oil in a heavy saucepan. Add the onions and sauté them gently until golden. Add the carrots and chicken broth. Simmer gently for 15 minutes until the carrots are soft and tender. Puree the soup in a food processor or blender, adding more broth if necessary to make the correct consistency. Reheat the soup. Season with salt and pepper and garnish with parsley or croutons.

Zucchini Eggplant Soup

Myrle Horn
Hollywood, Florida

Serves 6

1 medium-size eggplant, peeled and cut
   in 1-inch cubes
½ teaspoon salt
2 tablespoons butter
3 stalks celery, diced
2 medium-size green peppers,
   cut in ½-inch squares
2 medium-size zucchini, skin on,
   cut in 1-inch cubes
2 cups coarsely chopped tomatoes, skinned
   and seeds removed
1 quart fresh or canned chicken broth
½ teaspoon oregano
Salt
Freshly ground pepper
Romano or Parmesan cheese, grated,
   or thinly sliced imported Swiss
   cheese (optional)

Place the eggplant in a colander, sprinkle with the ½ teaspoon salt and let drain.
Heat the butter and sauté the celery and green peppers until nearly tender but still crisp. Pat the eggplant dry and add. Cook until tender. Add the zucchini and cook briefly, stirring. Add the tomatoes and stir well. Add the chicken broth and seasonings. Cook over medium heat for 30 minutes, stirring occasionally. Serve plain, or sprinkled lightly with grated Romano or Parmesan cheese, or with a slice of Swiss cheese placed on top of the soup in an ovenproof bowl. Run under the broiler until bubbly.

Artichoke, Egg and Lemon Soup
(Artichoke Avgolemono Soup)

Avgolemono is a piquant golden blend of eggs and lemon juice used extensively in Greek cooking and believed, by some food authorities, to be the predecessor of the famous French sauce called hollandaise. For this recipe, if you can get fresh baby artichokes, you can use them whole (since they have no choke) instead of the artichoke hearts. Alternatively, frozen artichokes are also acceptable, and depending on one's taste, the amount of lemon juice may be increased for a more pronounced lemon flavor.

L'Epicure School of Cooking
Rosa Rajkovic
Albuquerque, New Mexico

Serves 8

1 small onion, chopped
2 medium-size potatoes, peeled and cubed
2 stalks celery, thinly sliced
7 cups chicken broth
¾ pound artichoke hearts, cooked, drained
   and coarsely chopped
3 large eggs, at room temperature
Juice of 2 to 3 lemons
Salt
Freshly ground white pepper

Combine in a heavy non-aluminum 6-quart pot the onion, potatoes, celery and chicken broth. Bring to a boil and reduce heat. Cover and simmer for approximately 25 minutes or until the vegetables are cooked. Add the cooked artichoke hearts and heat through. Remove from the heat.

Separate the eggs and beat the whites until they hold soft peaks. Slowly beat in the egg yolks, one at a time, and the lemon juice. Take a ladle of liquid from the soup pot and slowly add it to the egg and lemon mixture, stirring constantly. Repeat with 2 more ladles of liquid, adding it very slowly, taking care not to curdle the egg mixture with the hot liquid. Briskly stir the contents of the bowl into the soup pot with a balloon whisk. Reduce heat to low and cook, whisking, until the soup thickens slightly. If it appears to start curdling around the edges of the pot, remove from the heat immediately and whisk rapidly. Fold in the egg white.

Season to taste with salt and pepper. Serve either hot or cold, garnished with lemon slices and chopped parsley.

Lentil Soup With Brie

Sally Flanzer
Little Rock, Arkansas

Serves 6

1 cup lentils
1 tablespoon butter
1 medium-size onion, diced
4 medium-size tomatoes,
   fresh or canned, chopped
1 cup diced carrot
1 cup diced celery
2 large cloves garlic, minced
2¼ cups chicken broth
1¼ cups beef broth
1 tablespoon Worcestershire sauce
1 tablespoon cider vinegar
4 black peppercorns, crushed
⅛ teaspoon thyme
1 bay leaf
6 wedges (1 ounce each) Brie cheese
Parsley for garnish

Rinse the lentils in a colander under warm running water. In a covered saucepan, bring them to a boil in 1½ quarts water. Remove from heat and let stand, covered, for 1 to 4 hours.

In a small skillet, heat the butter and lightly sauté the onion until limp but not brown.

In a soup pot, combine all the ingredients except the cheese and parsley, including the lentils and the water they have been soaking in. Simmer over low heat, uncovered, for 45 minutes.

Remove the bay leaf and puree the soup in a blender or food processor fitted with a knife blade, switching off when the mixture is still a little chunky. At this stage, the soup may be refrigerated, or even frozen.

To serve, heat the soup to piping hot. Place a wedge of the cheese in the bottom of each of 6 soup bowls and ladle the hot soup over the cheese. Garnish with sprigs of parsley.

Pumpkin Mushroom Soup

An unusual combination of ingredients makes this a particularly interesting soup. It can be garnished with freshly grated Parmesan cheese, chopped parsley or buttered croutons, rather than sour cream, if preferred.

Carmen Jones
Spring, Texas

Serves 5 to 6

8 tablespoons butter
1 pound mushrooms, sliced
1 large onion, chopped
⅓ cup flour
2 quarts chicken broth
2 cups cooked pumpkin, pureed
2 cups heavy cream
2 teaspoons honey
1 to 2 teaspoons curry powder
Salt
Freshly ground pepper
Sour cream for garnish

Heat the butter in a heavy stock pot and sauté the mushrooms over high heat until golden brown. Remove the mushrooms from the pot and add the onion. Sauté over medium heat until transparent. Add the flour and mix well. Cook until well done but not browned, 4 to 5 minutes. Add the chicken broth and the pumpkin, stir well and bring to a boil. Return the mushrooms to the soup and reduce the heat. Simmer for about 20 minutes. Add the cream, honey and curry powder, and cook another 10 minutes. Add salt and pepper to taste. Serve hot with sour cream on top.

Cucumber Egg Drop Soup

This simple soup is a fine beginning for either an oriental or an occidental dinner.

Shirley Waterloo
Hinsdale, Illinois

Serves 6

1 tablespoon peanut oil
¼-inch piece fresh ginger, finely minced
2½ quarts chicken broth
1 cucumber, peeled, scored, seeds removed
  and thinly sliced
1 egg, beaten with a fork
6 scallions, green parts only,
  thinly sliced

Heat the peanut oil in a large pot until almost smoking. Add the ginger and stir-fry until lightly browned, about half a minute. Add the chicken broth. Bring to a boil, reduce heat and simmer, covered, 30 minutes. Let stand in a cool place for several hours.

Bring the soup to a boil. Add the cucumber and simmer about 1 minute, uncovered, until the cucumber is tender. Bring to a boil again briefly, then reduce heat, and, quickly stirring with a chopstick or the handle of a wooden spoon, make a whirlpool in the center of the soup. Pour in the beaten egg slowly, then remove the pot from the heat. Divide the scallion slices among the 6 bowls and ladle the hot soup over the scallions. Serve at once.

Curried Crab Soup

Pat Opler
Hinsdale, Illinois and Wilson, Wyoming

Serves 6

4 tablespoons butter
1 medium-size onion, minced
2 tablespoons minced green pepper
3 tablespoons flour
2 tablespoons curry powder
½ teaspoon grated nutmeg
2 tablespoons tomato paste
8 cups milk
2 cups crabmeat, flaked
1 cup heavy cream or crème fraîche
Salt
Pepper
½ cup chopped chives

Heat the butter in a 6-quart saucepan. Add the onion and green pepper. Cook until the onion becomes transparent. Add the flour and cook 1 minute. Add the curry powder and nutmeg. Simmer 1 minute longer. Add the tomato paste and stir until smooth. Add the milk and stir until thickened. Add the crabmeat and the cream. Bring the soup just to a simmer. Season to taste with salt and pepper. Serve hot, sprinkled with chives.

Scandinavian Fruit Soup

World of Cuisine
Marcia R. Fox
Denver, Colorado

Serves 8 to 12

½ cup dried prunes
½ cup dried apricots
½ cup dried peaches
Zest of 1 lemon
½ cup canned plums, drained, juice reserved
½ cup canned sour pie cherries,
   drained, juice reserved
¼ cup sugar
2 teaspoons cornstarch
6 tablespoons dark rum
Sour cream (optional)

Place the dried fruits in a pot and add boiling water to cover. Leave to soak overnight.

Add the lemon zest to the pot with the fruit and cook the mixture over medium-low heat until the fruit is quite soft. Add the plums, cherries and ½ cup each of their juices and simmer for 5 minutes.

Meanwhile, combine the sugar, cornstarch and rum to make a paste. Add the paste to the soup and simmer 5 minutes more. Serve either hot or cold topped with sour cream.

Quick Cold Apricot Soup

Small meringues or macaroons go well with this soup.

Ursula's Cooking School
Ursula Knaeusel
Atlanta, Georgia

Serves 8

2 cans (16 ounces each) apricots,
   including peel and juice
1 cup sour cream
½ cup white wine
¼ cup apricot liqueur
2 tablespoons lemon juice
2 teaspoons vanilla extract
Powdered cinnamon

Blend all the ingredients together. Place the mixture in the freezer for 2 hours. Stir, sprinkle with cinnamon and serve at once.

Main Courses

No other section of this book more accurately reflects the diversity of approach, interest and technique to be found within the International Association of Cooking Schools than this eclectic collection of main course dishes. Consider the extent to which cooking styles and preferences differ regionally in the United States alone; from the East or the West, the North or the South, each tradition shows its unmistakable influence in these pages. The international origin of many of the dishes selected by our contributors brings a further interest to this part of the book, which is studded with the culinary enthusiasms of China, Hungary, Italy, Thailand, Germany, Mexico, India, France, Greece and Pakistan.

The range of meats, poultry and seafoods used here naturally reflects regional and national conditions of preference and availability, and it is interesting that the greatest number of dishes employ the use of chicken. This tells us something about the catholicity of a bird that is domestic everywhere and appreciated all over the world. In the United States, of course, the promise of "a chicken in every pot" once meant that prosperity was just around the corner. In these more cynical times, whatever may be around the corner, chicken remains the sought-after content for many pots.

This chapter offers recipes for all cooks, but every cook works under particular conditions. Some of these recipes are suitable when time, money and calories don't count; they will justify your effort and expenditure, but don't take any of them on when what you really want to do is something quick and easy. Under pressure from time and/or budget, pick one of the many recipes here that is designed to be economical in schedule and exchequer. Nor should you neglect the diet fare that's here; even when you aren't dieting, you'll find the results gratifying.

If you are new to the kitchen, start with simpler recipes and gradually establish confidence as you work up to complicated procedures, progressing at your own pace for your own full-scale cooking course.

Filet Marie Louise

Marina Polvay
Miami Shores, Florida

Serves 6
Preheat oven to 450 degrees

6 filet mignons
½ cup brandy
¼ teaspoon dried thyme
¼ teaspoon dried grated nutmeg
¼ teaspoon dried basil
¼ teaspoon freshly ground black pepper
Salt
Pepper
4 tablespoons clarified butter

PÂTÉ:
¼ cup minced scallions
¼ cup heavy cream
1-2 tablespoons minced truffles, or
   3 tablespoons minced sautéed mushrooms
1 cup pâté de foie gras (about 8 ounces)
Salt
Pepper

SAUCE:
4 tablespoons butter
6 shallots, minced
¼ cup dry sherry
Freshly ground black pepper
1 cup red wine
2 cloves garlic, minced
¼ teaspoon dried thyme
¼ teaspoon dried chervil
¼ cup brandy
Salt
3 tablespoons minced truffles

Sprinkle the filets on all sides with brandy and seasonings. Place them in a shallow dish, cover with foil and refrigerate until ready to use.

In a large skillet, heat the butter over medium-high heat and sauté the filets until browned on both sides to desired doneness. Remove from skillet and keep warm, saving the skillet drippings for the sauce.

Make the pâté: Mix all the pâté ingredients together in a smooth paste.

Make the sauce: Melt the butter in a saucepan and sauté the shallots until they are transparent, about 5 minutes. Deglaze the skillet in which the filets were sautéed, pouring in the sherry and scraping the bottom of the skillet with a wooden spoon; bring it to a boil and pour into the saucepan.

Add the pepper, red wine, garlic, thyme and chervil. Bring to a boil, reduce the heat, and cook the sauce, uncovered, until it is reduced by a quarter. Add the brandy and salt and cook, stirring occasionally, until slightly thickened.
Add the truffles and heat, but do not let it boil.

To serve, spoon 2 or 3 tablespoons of the sauce over each filet and pipe a rosette of the pâté on top.

Braised Steak Esterhazy

This Hungarian dish is traditionally served with hot buttered noodles.

Kenneth C. Wolfe
Lafayette, California

Serves 6
Preheat oven to 350 degrees

Salt
Freshly ground pepper
6 bottom round steaks, 8 ounces each
Flour for dredging
½ cup pork fat
2 large onions, cut in strips
4 stalks celery, cut in julienne strips
3 medium-size carrots, cut in julienne strips
1 teaspoon minced garlic
1 tablespoon tomato paste
2 to 3 cups beef broth
2 tablespoons flour
1 cup sour cream
2 tablespoons Dijon mustard
1 teaspoon anchovy paste
1 tablespoon capers, drained and chopped
3 dill pickles, cut in julienne strips

Salt and pepper the steaks and dredge in flour. Heat half of the fat in a heavy skillet and brown the meat quickly, about 1 minute on each side. Transfer to a flameproof casserole, slightly overlapping the steaks. Keep warm.

Add the remaining fat to the skillet and sauté the onions, celery, carrots and garlic for a few minutes. Drain off any excess fat, then add the tomato paste. Stir and simmer for a few minutes. Add 2 cups of the beef broth to the pan, stir and bring to a boil. Pour the mixture over the meat and cover the casserole. Bake in the preheated oven 45 minutes to 1 hour, until the meat is tender, checking occasionally and adding more broth if necessary to prevent the dish drying out.

Transfer the steaks to a heated serving platter and keep warm. Add a little water to the casserole, over heat, and scrape up any brown bits. Combine 2 tablespoons of flour with the sour cream, mixing well. Bring the liquid in the casserole to a boil and add the sour cream mixture; stir well and cook, stirring, 2 to 3 minutes. Do not let the mixture boil or the sour cream will separate. Add more beef broth if it seems too thick. Stir in the mustard, anchovy paste and capers. Mix well. Pour the sauce over the steaks, garnish with pickle strips and serve at once.

Steak Stuffed with Oysters

Nancy Coolidge
Fayetteville, North Carolina

Serves 6

SAUCE:
2 tablespoons butter
3 tablespoons minced shallots, or scallions
½ cup beef stock
½ cup dry red wine

12 select raw oysters
6 rib eye steaks, 8 ounces each,
   1 inch thick
Salt
Freshly ground pepper
1 tablespoon butter
2 tablespoons cognac
Chopped parsley for garnish

Prepare the sauce: Heat the butter in a small skillet, add the shallots and cook over low heat for about 5 minutes, until they have softened. Add the beef broth and the wine. Cook, uncovered, stirring occasionally, until the sauce is reduced by a third. Keep warm.

Plump the oysters: Put them in a saucepan and heat them slowly over low heat just until the edges curl slightly. Drain and keep warm.

Sprinkle the steaks with salt and pepper. About 15 minutes before serving time, heat the butter in a large heavy skillet over medium-high heat. Add the steaks and fry for 3 to 4 minutes on each side for medium-rare. Remove the pan from the heat and add the brandy and flame it. After the flames have died down, remove the meat from the pan and cut a pocket in each steak. Stuff each with 2 oysters. Put the steak on a warm platter.

Add the sauce to the skillet in which the steaks were cooked and bring it to a boil, stirring. Ladle the sauce over the steaks, sprinkle with the chopped parsley and serve at once.

Stuffed Spencer Steak

These steak-stuffed steaks are best cooked over hot coals in the great outdoors, but broiling them in the kitchen can also prove quite satisfactory.

Inner Gourmet Cooking School
Pasadena, California

Serves 8

1 pound ground round steak
3 tablespoons green peppercorns
1½ teaspoons garlic salt
1 teaspoon lemon pepper
1 tablespoon chopped parsley
4 Spencer steaks, about ¾ inch thick,
   butterflied
¼ cup melted butter
Juice of 1-2 lemons

   Mix the ground round steak, green peppercorns, garlic salt, lemon pepper and parsley together in a bowl. Stuff one quarter of the mixture into each butterflied steak and skewer each one closed. Grill for 4 to 5 minutes for each side, then immediately pour a little melted butter and fresh lemon juice over each steak. Serve hot.

Sliced Steak with Garlic and Olive Sauce

The steaks may be cooked over a barbecue if preferred.

Myrle Horn
Hollywood, Florida

Serves 4
Preheat the broiler

1 flank steak, about 2 pounds
¼ cup Worcestershire sauce
Freshly ground pepper

SAUCE:
1 cup butter
8 cloves garlic, coarsely chopped
1 cup pimiento-stuffed green olives,
   coarsely chopped

   Score the top of the steak to prevent it curling during cooking. Cover the meat with the Worcestershire sauce and a good grinding of pepper. Leave to marinate for 1 hour.
   Heat the butter in a heavy saucepan and add the garlic and olives. Cook over low heat until bubbly. Keep warm.
   Remove the meat from the marinade and broil it on the second level under the broiler, to the desired degree of doneness. Discard the marinade. Slice the meat across the grain and arrange the slices on a warm serving platter. Pour the sauce over the meat and serve immediately.

Mongolian Beef, Mandarin Style

Oriental Food Market and Cooking School
Chu Yen and Pansy Luke
Chicago, Illinois

Serves 4

1 pound flank steak
MARINADE:
1½ tablespoons light soy sauce
1 large egg, lightly beaten
2 tablespoons cornstarch

1½ tablespoons light soy sauce
1 teaspoon salt
½ teaspoon sugar
1 teaspoon sesame oil
2-3 cups peanut oil, or vegetable oil
1 package rice stick noodles
3 or 4 dried hot red peppers, broken in pieces
   and soaked in water for ½ hour
10 scallions in 1½-inch slices cut on the bias

Put the flank steak in the freezer and leave it until it is firm, about half an hour. Meanwhile mix the marinade ingredients in a bowl.

In a separate bowl combine the 1½ tablespoons soy sauce, salt, sugar and sesame oil, and set aside.

Slice the meat thinly, no more than 1/16 inch thick, and cut the slices into pieces about 1½ inches long. Place in the marinade. Mix well, then leave for about half an hour. Drain the meat and discard the marinade.

Heat the oil in a wok to about 400 degrees. Loosen the rice stick noodles and deep-fry them briefly — for only a couple of seconds — on one side, then turn them and fry on the other side for an even shorter time. Remove and drain well on paper towels. Crush the noodles slightly, and arrange on a heated serving platter.

Lower the temperature of the oil to 375 degrees. Deep-fry the beef for half a minute. Remove from the wok with a slotted spoon or Chinese strainer and set aside.

Remove all the oil from the wok except about 1½ tablespoons. Heat the oil until it smokes. Add the red peppers and scallions and stir-fry quickly for a moment or two. Return the beef to the wok and pour in the soy sauce mixture. Mix well, and spoon the mixture onto the bed of fried rice stick noodles. Serve immediately.

Bourbon Beef

This dish may be made ahead and reheated, but should not be frozen. Serve with buttered noodles or parsleyed new potatoes.

Kay's School of Cookery
Kathryn Domurot
Pittsburgh, Pennsylvania

Serves 4

1 tablespoon flour
½ teaspoon salt
½ teaspoon freshly ground pepper
2 pounds round steak, cut 1½ inches thick
2 tablespoons solid shortening, or vegetable oil
2 large onions, diced
¼ cup bourbon whiskey
1 to 1½ cups tomato juice
1 to 1½ cups dry white wine
Chopped parsley for garnish

Mix together the flour, salt and pepper. Place the meat on a cutting board and sprinkle half the mixture on one side. With a mallet or the side of a cleaver, pound the seasoned flour into the meat, flattening it as much as possible. Turn the meat over and repeat.

Heat the shortening in a Dutch oven or a heavy pan with a cover, and brown the pounded meat well on both sides. Upending the meat at one side of the pan, add the onions and cook them, stirring, until golden colored. Lay the meat down again.

Pour the bourbon over the browned meat and onions and light it with a match. As soon as the flame dies down, add 1 cup of the the tomato juice and 1 cup of the wine. Cover the pan and reduce the heat to low. Simmer for 1½ hours, or until the beef is fork-tender, checking and adding tomato juice and/or wine if the liquid is reducing too much.

Cut the meat into slices about ¼ inch thick and transfer to a heated serving dish. Cover with the sauce and garnish with parsley. Serve at once.

Steaks with Shallot-Cream Sauce

Dorothy Crebo
Kokomo, Indiana

Serves 4

2 tablespoons vegetable oil
2 to 3 tablespoons butter
4 rib eye steaks, 1¼ inches thick
2 tablespoons minced shallots
½ cup strong beef broth
½ cup good brandy
½ cup heavy cream
Salt
Freshly ground pepper

Heat the oil and 2 tablespoons of the butter in a large heavy skillet until very hot. Sauté the steaks until nicely browned and medium-rare, about 5 minutes each side. Remove to a heated serving platter and keep warm.

Add butter to the skillet if needed, and sauté the shallots for about 1 minute. Add the beef broth and the brandy. Raise the heat and stir, scraping the brown bits from the bottom. Continue to cook over high heat, uncovered, until reduced by half. Lower the heat. Add the cream and cook, stirring, until the sauce thickens. Season to taste with salt and pepper. Pour the sauce over the steaks and serve immediately.

Chinese Beef with Tomato and Green Pepper

Serve this dish with rice.

Catherine Kunkle
New Richmond, Wisconsin

Serves 4

1-pound sirloin steak
MARINADE:
1 clove garlic, minced
1 slice fresh ginger, minced
2 tablespoons dark soy sauce
1 tablespoon dry sherry
1 teaspoon sugar
1 teaspoon cornstarch

2 teaspoons fermented black beans, rinsed
1 clove garlic, minced
1 slice fresh ginger, minced
1 tablespoon cornstarch
1 teaspoon dark soy sauce
1 tablespoon tomato paste
1 cup chicken broth
4 tablespoons peanut oil
1 large green pepper, seeded and
    cut in short strips
1 medium-size onion, cut in
    16 triangular wedges
¼ pound fresh mushrooms, sliced
1 large ripe tomato, cut in 16 triangular
    wedges, seeds discarded

Cut the beef across the grain into slices ⅛ inch thick. Combine the marinade ingredients, cover the beef with the mixture and marinate 30 minutes to 12 hours.

Combine the black beans with the garlic and ginger. In another bowl, combine the cornstarch, dark soy sauce, tomato paste and chicken broth.

Heat an empty wok to smoking. Add 2 tablespoons of the peanut oil. When the oil is very hot, add the beef and stir-fry over high heat until browned. Remove and keep warm. Add the leftover marinade to the cornstarch mixture. Mix well. Add the rest of the oil to the wok. When it is hot, add the black bean mixture and stir-fry for half a minute. Add the green pepper, onion, mushrooms and tomato, in that order, stir-frying constantly. Add the cornstarch mixture and continue to stir-fry until the sauce has thickened and is clear. Return the beef to the wok, stir-fry just long enough to get it very hot, and serve at once.

Sauerbraten

This may be served with potato dumplings for a traditional and extra-hearty meal.

Cloudtree & Sun
Joanne E. Stoney
Gresham, Oregon

Serves 6
Preheat oven to 325 degrees

MARINADE:
1 cup vinegar
1 medium-size onion, chopped
¼ cup sugar
1 tablespoon pickling spices,
 tied in cheesecloth
1 stick cinnamon
1 teaspoon salt
¼ teaspoon freshly ground pepper

1 chuck roast, 4 pounds
8 gingersnaps, crumbled
2 tablespoons brown sugar
Dash of ground cinnamon

Combine the marinade ingredients with 2 cups of water. Pour over the roast in a container made of ceramic or glass (not metal). Cover and refrigerate overnight. Put the meat with its marinade in a Dutch oven or heavy baking pan with a cover. Bake, covered, in the preheated oven for 2 hours.

Put the crumbled gingersnaps into ¼ cup boiling water in a heavy saucepan. Stir well, adding the brown sugar and the ground cinnnamon.

Remove the roast from the oven and keep warm. Skim off any extra grease from the surface of the liquid in the baking pan, then strain it into the saucepan with the gingersnap mixture. Cook, stirring, over low heat, until well mixed and very hot. Slice the meat and arrange the slices on a heated serving platter. Pour a little of the sauce from the saucepan over the slices and the rest into a sauceboat, to pass separately.

Stuffed Eye of Round

Bain-Marie
Dolly Hlava
Pearland, Texas

Serves 8 to 10
Preheat oven to 300 degrees

1 eye-of-round roast, 4 to 5 pounds
1 pound chorizo or hot Italian sausages
¼ pound smoked bacon, cut in pieces
¼ cup pimiento-stuffed green olives, sliced
¼ cup olive oil
1 large apple, peeled, cored and chopped
2 large onions, chopped
1 stalk celery, chopped
½ small green pepper, seeded and chopped
1 large tomato, peeled and quartered,
  seeds discarded
½ teaspoon dried oregano
1 bay leaf
1 teaspoon salt
½ teaspoon freshly ground pepper
½ cup red wine

Cut a pocket through the center of the roast, lengthwise. Remove all the sausage from its casings and crumble into a skillet. Cook for a few minutes and remove to a bowl with a slotted spoon. Pour off the fat from the skillet and put the bacon in to fry lightly. Transfer with a slotted spoon to the bowl with the sausage and add the olives. Mix well, and stuff the roast evenly with the mixture. Close the ends of the roast with skewers to enclose the stuffing.

Heat the olive oil in a heavy roasting pan that has a cover. Sear the roast on all sides in the oil. Remove from the pan. Add all the other ingredients except the wine, and sauté the mixture, stirring occasionally, until the onion is transparent. Put the roast back in the pan, add the wine, cover and bake in the preheated oven about 2 hours, basting and turning the meat from time to time.

Remove the meat from the pan onto a warm serving platter to rest for 10 minutes before slicing. Skim excess fat from the roasting pan and transfer the contents to a blender or food processor and puree. Reheat, and serve as a sauce over the meat slices, or passed in a sauceboat.

Veal Alla Romana

A risotto with grated Parmesan is good with this, or hot cooked noodles tossed with thin strips of lightly-colored zucchini. With sausage added, this also goes well with spaghetti.

Libby Hillman's Cooking School
Libby Hillman
Great Neck, New York and Whittingham, Vermont

Serves 8
Preheat oven to 350 degrees

3 to 4 pounds boned shoulder of veal,
  cut into 1½-inch cubes
1 teaspoon coarse salt
2 tablespoons butter
1 pound fresh mushrooms, sliced
¼ cup olive oil
1 cup tomato puree
1 cup chicken broth or veal broth
½ cup Madeira wine
2 tablespoons lemon juice
1 tablespoon minced garlic
½ teaspoon dried thyme
1½ tablespoons chopped parsley, preferably
  Italian parsley
1 teaspoon freshly ground pepper
Salt (optional)

Toss the veal with the coarse salt. Heat the butter in a large skillet and sauté the mushrooms. When lightly cooked, transfer to a Dutch oven or a heavy casserole with a close-fitting cover.

Add the olive oil to the skillet and brown the veal pieces a few at a time. When well browned, transfer to the casserole. Add the tomato puree, broth, wine, lemon juice, garlic, thyme, 1 teaspoon of the parsley, and the pepper, and mix well. Place a greased sheet of foil directly over the surface of the food and cover the pan tightly. Bake in the preheated oven 1 hour, or until the meat is tender. Taste and add salt, if necessary, and serve hot, garnished with the remaining parsley.

Calf's Liver in Oyster Sauce

Calf's liver is delicious cooked in this Chinese style with oyster sauce.

Jean Yueh
Summit, New Jersey

Serves 4

1 pound calf's liver, thinly sliced
2 pieces fresh ginger, roughly ½-inch cubes
2 teaspoons cornstarch
¼ teaspoon freshly ground black pepper

SAUCE:
2 tablespoons dry sherry
2 tablespoons soy sauce
2 tablespoons oyster sauce
2 teaspoons sugar
2 teaspoons cornstarch

6 tablespoons peanut oil, or vegetable oil
2 medium-size onions, peeled and halved,
  then sliced
2 teaspoons seasame oil (optional)

Remove any membrane and veins from the liver and cut the slices into pieces about 2 inches by 3 inches. Place in a bowl. Put the ginger in a garlic press and squeeze the ginger juice over the liver. Add the cornstarch and pepper to the bowl. Mix well.

Mix the sauce ingredients in another bowl and set aside. Heat 1 tablespoon of the oil in a wok or deep skillet. Stir-fry the onions for a minute or two, until light golden in color but still crisp. Remove from the wok and reserve.

Add the remaining oil to the wok and heat. When the oil is very hot, add the liver. Quickly spread the pieces of liver over the surface of the wok so that there is no overlapping, and brown. Turn them to brown the other side, cooking no more than a total time of 2 minutes, so the inner part of the liver will still be pink. Spoon from the wok to a sieve or colander, and shake slightly to drain. Drain the wok.

Return the onion and the liver to the wok. Add the sauce ingredients and stir-fry until the sauce thickens and coats the liver. Remove from the heat and stir in the sesame oil, if desired. Serve at once.

Lamb Chops en Papillote

For this you will need six large heart-shaped pieces of parchment paper, one for each lamb chop. If large lamb chops are not readily available, twelve small ones will do just as well, with the number and size of the parchment hearts adjusted accordingly.

Zona Spray Cooking School
Zona Spray
Hudson, Ohio

Serves 6
Preheat oven to 450 degrees

6 large loin lamb chops, ¾ to 1 inch thick
Salt
Freshly ground pepper
7 tablespoons Madeira wine
6 thin slices prosciutto, or boiled ham
3 to 6 tablespoons clarified butter
10 fresh mushrooms, minced
1 clove garlic, finely chopped
4 tablespoons minced shallots
4 tablespoons tomato sauce, or peeled,
  seeded, chopped tomatoes
Pinch of dried tarragon
Pinch of dried basil
Pinch of ground nutmeg
¾ cup beef broth
1½ tablespoons butter
1½ tablespoons flour
2 cups rice
6 slices, 3 inches by 3 inches, Gruyère
  or Swiss cheese

Pat the lamb chops with paper towels and season with salt and pepper. Heat 3 tablespoons of the Madeira in a small skillet and heat the proscuitto slices, separately, very quickly, only

about 10 seconds for each slice. Remove from the skillet and keep warm.

Heat the clarified butter in a large heavy skillet and sauté the chops for about 2 minutes on each side, or until browned but still very rare on the inside. Transfer to a warm platter.

Add the mushrooms, garlic and shallots to the skillet and cook until the shallots are almost transparent. Add the tomato sauce or tomatoes, tarragon, basil and nutmeg, and season with salt and pepper. Add the beef broth and cook over high heat until the liquid has reduced by about a third. Combine the butter and flour to make a beurre manie. Add 4 tablespoons of Madeira to the pan and bring it to a boil. Stir in the beurre manié, a little at a time, until the sauce is thick and smooth. Take the pan off the heat and adjust the seasonings.

Butter a heart-shaped piece of parchment and lay it on a flat surface. Place on it in layers, first ⅓ cup of rice, then a half slice of cheese, then a lamb chop, some sauce and another half slice of cheese; top with the prosciutto or boiled ham. Crimp the paper edges shut. Repeat the process with the other chops.

Bake on a baking sheet in a single layer in the preheated oven for 10 minutes or until the paper puffs. Serve immediately on individual plates, and let each person cut the heart open and eat from the paper.

Steamed Leg of Lamb with Garden Vegetables

For this a large double-level steamer is required. The two heads of garlic for the steaming water may seem like too much, but they are not.

The Silo
Douglas Spingler
New Milford, Connecticut

Serves 8

1 leg of lamb, about 6 pounds
2 heads garlic
2 tablespoons fresh thyme
2 tablespoons fennel seed
2 tablespoons fresh rosemary
3 or 4 bay leaves
1 teaspoon black peppercorns
8 or 10 small fresh beets, peeled
1 small head cauliflower, cut into florets
1 or 2 small eggplants, diced
8 to 10 white onions, peeled
8 to 10 baby carrots, scrubbed
8 small zucchini
8 small yellow squash

SAUCE:
1 quart lamb broth
1 clove garlic, minced
1 tablespoon chopped fresh mint
1 tablespoon chopped fresh parsley
1 tablespoon fresh rosemary
1 tablespoon fresh thyme
1 teaspoon chopped lavender leaves (optional)
Mixed chopped fresh herbs for garnish (optional)

Trim the meat of fat and cut it to fit in the steamer basket. (Any meaty trimmings can be used in making the lamb broth for the sauce.)

Fill the bottom of the steamer pan with water and put over high heat. Add the garlic, thyme, fennel seed, rosemary, bay leaves and peppercorns. Bring the water to a boil, then reduce heat and simmer, covered, for 20 minutes.

Place the lamb in the first basket of the steamer and cover. Steam for about 1½ hours, to become medium-rare. After it has steamed 1 hour, begin adding the vegetables to the top basket of the steamer, according to cooking time. Add the beets and cauliflower first, to steam 30 minutes. Ten minutes later, add the eggplant and onions, to steam 20 minutes. Five minutes later, add the carrots, to steam 15 minutes. After 5 more minutes, add the zucchini and yellow squash, to steam 10 minutes. The water level in the steamer will need checking, and water added if needed.

Meanwhile make the sauce: Put the sauce ingredients in a heavy saucepan. Bring to a boil, reduce and simmer, uncovered, until reduced by half. Strain and keep hot.

Place the lamb on a heated serving platter and press some chopped fresh herbs onto the surface of the meat, if desired. Let the meat rest about 10 minutes before slicing. Serve with the vegetables, and the sauce.

Pakistani Lamb with Spinach

Serve with a rice pilaf.

Loni Kuhn
San Francisco, California

Serves 8

3 pounds fresh spinach
3 medium-size onions, chopped coarsely
2 cloves garlic, minced
2-inch piece fresh ginger
1 fresh jalapeño pepper
½ cup vegetable oil
3 pounds lean boneless lamb, cut into
    1-inch cubes
3-inch cinnamon stick, broken in pieces
7 whole cardamom pods
7 whole cloves
2 bay leaves
2 tablespoons ground coriander
1 tablespoon ground cumin
1½ teaspoons ground turmeric
2 tomatoes, peeled and chopped
1¼ cups yogurt
Salt

Cook the spinach, drain and squeeze it to remove all the liquid. Chop the spinach finely.

Place the onion, garlic, ginger and jalapeño pepper in a food processor and process until smooth.

Heat the oil in a large, heavy pan and brown the meat a few pieces at a time. Remove the meat from the pan.

Add the cinnamon, cardamom, cloves and bay leaves to the pan and cook for 1 minute.

Add the onion mixture. Mix well and cook, stirring constantly, for about 10 minutes. Add the coriander, cumin and turmeric and cook for 2 minutes more. Return the meat to the pan and stir in the spinach and tomatoes, and 2 tablespoons of the yogurt. Bring to a boil, lower the heat, cover and simmer gently for about 45 minutes. Taste for seasoning, and add salt if needed. Serve with additional yogurt.

Eggplant Rolls Stuffed with Lamb
(Roulades aux Aubergines)

Serve with rice pilaf and a good tossed salad.

Beryl Marton
Ogunquit, Maine

Serves 8
Preheat oven to 350 degrees

4 to 6 tablespoons vegetable oil
2 pounds stewing lamb, trimmed and
   cut in cubes
1 clove garlic, minced
2 large onions, chopped
1 cup dry red wine
2 cups beef broth
1 teaspoon salt
Freshly ground pepper
1 eggplant, 1½ to 2 pounds, peeled
½ pound mushrooms, chopped
1 teaspoon ground cinnamon
¼ teaspoon ground allspice
4 tablespoons butter
4 tablespoons flour
Chopped parsley for garnish

Heat 1 tablespoon of the oil in a medium-sized Dutch oven or heavy pan with a lid. Brown the meat quickly on all sides. Remove from the pan and drain on paper towels. Add the garlic and half the onions to the pan. Sauté until the onion is limp. Return the meat to the pan and add the wine, broth, salt and pepper. Bring to a boil, stirring. Lower the heat and simmer, covered, 1½ hours. Drain the meat and refrigerate the cooking liquid.

Chop the meat finely and set aside. When the broth has cooled thoroughly, remove the grease from the surface, and measure 2 cups of liquid, or add water to make it 2 cups.

Slice about 1 inch off each end of the peeled eggplant and mince. Cut the remaining eggplant into 16 thin slices. Heat 3 tablespoons of the oil in a skillet and sauté the eggplant slices until limp, adding more oil as needed. Drain well on paper towels.

Add the chopped onion to the skillet and sauté until limp. Add the minced eggplant, mushrooms, cinnamon and allspice. Cook, stirring constantly, for 5 minutes. Add the chopped lamb and mix well. Taste for seasoning and add salt and pepper if needed.

Grease a shallow baking dish. Place a large spoonful of lamb mixture in the center of each eggplant slice, and roll the eggplant up around it. Place, seam side down, in the baking dish. Bake in the preheated oven for 15 to 20 minutes, or until well heated through.

Meanwhile make the sauce: In a saucepan bring the reserved 2 cups of pan juices slowly to a boil. In another saucepan, heat the butter, and when it foams, add the flour. Cook, stirring, for 2 minutes. Remove from the heat, pour in the boiling liquid from the other saucepan, and beat vigorously with a whisk. Return the pan to the heat and cook for 2 to 3 minutes, until the sauce thickens. Adjust the seasonings.

Serve the eggplant rolls hot, garnished with chopped parsley and accompanied with the sauce.

Shish Kebab Valger

Serve the shish kebab with saffron rice, caesar salad, crusty bread and a fine and mellow burgundy.

The Uncomplicated Gourmet
Nancy Stern
Westwood, New Jersey

Serves 6

MARINADE:
Juice of 2 large lemons
2 tablespoons grated onion
4 tablespoons olive oil
2 tablespoons dried chili pepper, crushed
1 teaspoon ground coriander
1 teaspoon ground ginger
2 cloves garlic, crushed
2 teaspoons Madras curry powder
2 teaspoons salt

2 pounds lamb from the leg,
   trimmed and cut in 2-inch cubes
3 large onions, peeled and quartered
2 green peppers, seeded and cut
   into 8 pieces each
12 cherry tomatoes
12 fresh mushrooms

Combine all the marinade ingredients and pour over the lamb cubes in a large, shallow pan. Refrigerate for 24 hours, turning the lamb occasionally.

Preheat the grill or broiler. Thread the lamb pieces on skewers, not too tightly. Set aside. Reserve the marinade.

Put a large pot of water over high heat. When boiling, drop the onion quarters in and cook 3 minutes. Remove with a slotted spoon and rinse under cold water. Drop the green pepper pieces into the water and cook 1 minute. Remove with a slotted spoon and rinse under cold water. Drain the onions and peppers well, and thread on skewers, alternating with the tomatoes and whole mushrooms.

Put all the skewers on the grill over hot coals, or in the broiler. Turn the vegetable skewers frequently. They will be done before the meat. Turn the meat every 5 minutes. Cook for about 20 minutes. As they grill, baste the meat and vegetables frequently with the reserved marinade. Serve on their skewers.

Lamb Shanks with Honey and Almonds

Elizabeth V. Thomas
Berkeley, California

Serves 4
Preheat oven to 450 degrees

SEASONING MIXTURE:
½ teaspoon crumbled saffron threads
1½ teaspoons ground cinnamon
½ teaspoon ground ginger
½ teaspoon salt
Freshly ground pepper
3 tablespoons all-purpose flour

4 lamb shanks, 5 to 5½ pounds
2 cups red wine
½ cup honey
½ cup slivered almonds

Mix together the seasoning mixture ingredients and rub into the lamb. Place the meat in a flameproof casserole or roasting pan and roast, uncovered, in the preheated oven 15 minutes. Turn the meat pieces over and roast 15 minutes longer.

Add the wine and the honey to the roasting pan and place over heat. Bring to a boil, stirring. Cover the pan and return it to the oven. Reduce the oven temperature to 300 degrees and cook for 1½ to 2 hours longer, until the meat is very tender. Meanwhile put the almonds in a shallow baking dish in one layer, and toast them in the same oven until they become light brown in color. Remove from the oven and reserve.

Remove the cooked lamb to a warm serving dish. Put the roasting pan over high heat, and reduce the pan juices until they have the consistency of syrup. Taste and adjust the seasonings. Pour the sauce over the meat, scatter the almonds over the top and serve immediately.

Grilled Butterflied Leg of Lamb

This is a dish to be cooked over charcoal. It will be good cold as well as hot, in the unlikely event that there is any left over.

Anne Byrd
Charlotte, North Carolina

Serves 6 to 8

**1 leg of lamb, about 6 pounds,
  boned and "butterflied"**

MARINADE:
⅔ cup lemon juice
⅓ cup dry vermouth
¼ cup olive oil
¼ cup Worcestershire sauce
4 cloves garlic, minced
1 tablespoon dried rosemary
1 teaspoon salt
1 teaspoon freshly ground black pepper
⅔ cup Dijon mustard
1 tablespoon dried rosemary

Trim any excess fat from the lamb. Combine the marinade ingredients, and mix well. Place the lamb in the marinade and leave for 24 hours, turning occasionally.

Prepare the charcoal grill. Drain the meat. Sprinkle the dried rosemary over the lighted coals to add flavor to the smoke. Brush the leg of lamb with mustard to coat it. Spread the lamb on a rack over medium-hot coals, and grill for 20 minutes. Baste the surface of the meat with half the marinade. Turn it and baste the other side with the other half of the marinade. Grill for about 20 minutes more. Remove the meat from the grill. Let rest for 10 minutes, then carve into thin slices and serve hot.

Pork Noisettes with Grapefruit

The glace de viande, which is optional in this recipe, can be purchased frozen in many specialty food shops.

Chez Deborah
Deborah Mefferd
Evergreen, Colorado

Serves 4

2 pork tenderloins
3 grapefruits
4 tablespoons sugar
3 tablespoons butter
1 onion, chopped
2 carrots, diced
3 stalks celery, chopped
½ teaspoon dried thyme
2 tablespoons cognac
2 tablespoons Madeira wine
1 tablespoon glace de viande (optional)
1 teaspoon arrowroot dissolved in
   1 tablespoon Madeira (optional)
Salt
Freshly ground black pepper

Cut each tenderloin into 12 noisettes, or small steaks, about 1¼ inches thick. Pat the meat well with paper towels and set aside at room temperature.

Carefully cut the zest thinly from 2 of the grapefruits, and put in a saucepan with the sugar and ½ cup of water. Bring to a boil and cook until the liquid is reduced by half. Pour it off and reserve. Continue cooking the zest in the pan until it nearly burns. Rinse the zest in cold water and reserve for garnishing.

Squeeze the juice from the same 2 grapefruits. Cut the zest from the third grapefruit and reserve. Then cut all the white pith from the flesh and cut the flesh from the membranes in sections as neatly as possible, for garnishing. Refrigerate.

Heat the butter and sauté the onion, carrots, celery and thyme together with the zest from the third grapefruit, cooking until the vegetables start to brown. Remove the mixture from the skillet and reserve. Raise the heat under the same skillet and sear the pork noisettes quickly on both sides. Return the vegetable mixture to the pan and add a few tablespoons of the grapefruit juice. Lower the heat and cook slowly about 15 minutes or until the noisettes are firm to the touch. Carefully remove the meat from the pan and keep warm. Add to the vegetables in the skillet the remaining grapefruit juice, the reserved sugar syrup, the cognac, Madeira and glace de viande (if including). Boil together until the sauce mixture has reduced somewhat. Pour it through a sieve into a clean saucepan, pressing the vegetables to extract all their liquid, then discarding them. Skim off all the fat from the surface of this sauce, and add salt and pepper to taste. If a thicker sauce is desired, add the arrowroot dissolved in wine, heat gently and stir until thickened.

Arrange the noisettes on a heated serving platter and spoon the sauce over them. Garnish with the reserved grapefruit sections and reserved zest.

Roast Pork in Flaky Crust

In the last stage of the preparation of this dish, the filo-encased pork may wait, covered with a damp towel, for a time before the final baking, if desired.

Donna Adams
New York, New York and Cleveland, Ohio

Serves 8
Preheat oven to 350 degrees

5- to 6- pound pork loin, boned
1 cup chicken broth
2 cloves garlic, crushed
2 teaspoons dried rosemary
10 tablespoons butter
2 medium-size onions, chopped
1 to 3 tablespoons Dijon mustard
1 cup heavy cream
2 tablespoons vegetable oil
10 sheets filo dough

Roast the pork loin on a rack in the preheated oven until a meat thermometer inserted in the center of the meat registers 185 degrees. Remove from oven, cool to room temperature and cut into ½-inch slices, retaining the shape of the loin as much as possible after slicing. Trim off any fat.

In a heavy saucepan, simmer together the chicken broth, garlic and rosemary, uncovered, for 20 minutes, then strain and return to the saucepan.

Heat 2 teaspoons of the butter in a skillet and sauté the onions until they are soft. Add to the liquid in the saucepan, and whisk in the mustard, to taste, and the cream. Simmer, uncovered, 15 minutes. Pour into a blender or food processor and blend. This mixture is to be used as a paste, to hold the slices of pork together, so if the mixture seems too thin, return it to the saucepan and cook to reduce it slightly. Spread it between the slices of pork and reform the shape of the loin. Put in a cool place.

Preheat the oven to 400 degrees. Heat the remaining butter with the oil. Grease a 10-by-15-inch jelly roll pan with shortening, and lay one sheet of the filo dough down in the pan. Brush it thoroughly with the melted butter and oil mixture. Lay another sheet on top and repeat. Continue until all 10 sheets are layered and buttered.

Place the assembled pork roast at one end of the top sheet of the filo. Roll all the layers with the roast, one turn. Tuck in the sides of the filo and continue rolling as for a strudel. Place, seam side down, in the jelly roll pan. Brush the surface with the rest of the butter mixture and bake in the preheated oven 20 to 25 minutes, until well browned.

Chicken with White Peaches

A rice pilaf is the recommended accompaniment for this dish.

Sue Sutker's Creative Cookery, Maas Brothers
Sue Sutker
Tampa, Florida

Serves 6
Preheat the oven to 350 degrees

2½-3 pounds chicken, cut in serving pieces
½ cup all-purpose flour
Salt
Freshly ground pepper
3 tablespoons unsalted butter
¼ cup vegetable oil
½ cup dry white wine or dry vermouth
1 bouquet garni (thyme, bay leaf and parsley
   tied in cheesecloth)
15-ounce can white peaches, drained
¼ cup dry sherry
¼ cup brandy for flaming

Mix the flour, salt and pepper, and roll the chicken pieces in the mixture, or shake them in a bag with the mixture to coat each piece lightly.

Heat the butter and oil together in a large frying pan, and brown the chicken pieces on all sides. Transfer them to a shallow casserole or ovenproof serving dish. Pour the wine or vermouth into the frying pan and stir over high heat to scrape up the brown bits. Pour the wine from the frying pan over the chicken in the casserole, and add the bouquet garni. Cover and bake in the preheated oven 45 minutes. (At this stage, the cooked chicken may be cooled and then refrigerated, covered, overnight, in which case it will be necessary to preheat the oven again to 350 degrees before the final baking.)

Discard the bouquet garni. Spoon the peaches carefully into the casserole, arranging them among the chicken pieces. Stir the sherry into the pan juices. Return the casserole to the oven, cover and bake for another 20 minutes.

Heat the brandy slightly. A moment before serving, flame the brandy and immediately pour it over the chicken and peaches. Carry the dish, flaming, to the table.

Poached Ham Mousselines
(Mousselines de Jambon)

Lois Lee
Minneapolis, Minnesota

Serves 6 to 8
Preheat oven to 400 degrees

½ pound ham, diced
½ pound veal, diced
¼ cup heavy cream
1 egg white, lightly beaten
Salt
Freshly ground white pepper

SAUCE:
1 egg yolk
¼ cup heavy cream
2 tablespoons butter
2 tablespoons flour

Truffle slices for garnish (optional)

Puree together the ham and the veal in a food processor, then press them through a sieve or food mill until absolutely smooth. Put the meat in a bowl and add the cream, a little at a time. Add the egg white and salt and pepper. Place the bowl over another bowl filled with ice, and beat the mixture with a wooden spoon until absolutely smooth. Using two spoons, form the mixture into small ovals and place them in a buttered shallow baking dish. Carefully pour boiling water into the baking dish to a depth of 1 inch. Cover the baking dish with buttered parchment paper and bake in the preheated oven 25 to 30 minutes.

Meanwhile, make the sauce: Beat the egg yolk and cream together. Heat the butter in a heavy saucepan and when it foams, stir in the flour. Cook together, stirring, 1 minute. Add ¼ cup boiling water and whisk until smooth and thickened. Remove from the heat. Carefully beat in the egg yolk mixture.

Season to taste with salt and pepper and cook gently until very hot throughout.

Serve the poached mousselines with the sauce spooned over them and truffle slices decorating the top, if desired.

Chinese Red-Cooked Chicken

Unlike most Chinese dishes, this one can be completely cooked the day before and simply reheated before serving. It can also be made with beef, or lamb, instead of chicken, and is particularly successful for less tender meats.

Deen Terry
Atlanta, Georgia

3 tablespoons peanut oil or vegetable oil
2 to 3 pounds chicken legs and thighs,
    cut through the bone into small pieces
2 tablespoons dry sherry
3 tablespoons soy sauce
1 teaspoon sugar
2 slices fresh ginger
3 scallions, cut in 1-inch pieces,
    or 1 small onion, sliced
2 star anise

Heat the oil in a deep pan until very hot. Sauté the chicken pieces, stirring, over medium-high heat for about 2 minutes. Add the remaining ingredients to the pan. Bring to a boil. Reduce the heat, cover and simmer for about 1 hour, stirring frequently. Serve with plain boiled rice.

The Sultan's Curried Chicken with Peanut Sauce

This dish may be made ahead of time and reheated in a moderate oven for twenty minutes before serving. Serve it on a bed of saffron rice.

Lee Ehudin
Lutherville, Maryland

Serves 4 to 6

¼ cup peanut oil
3 pounds chicken breasts, skinned
1 medium-size onion, minced
1 clove garlic, minced
½ teaspoon sugar
½ teaspoon salt
1 tablespoon chopped fresh parsley
1 cinnamon stick, broken in four pieces
1 tablespoon curry powder
¾ teaspoon ground ginger
2 large tomatoes, skinned and chopped, or
    16-ounce can tomatoes, cut up
½ cup peanut butter

Heat the oil in a large, heavy skillet. Brown the chicken pieces briefly, then remove from the pan and keep warm. Add the onion and garlic and cook until softened. Add the sugar, salt, parsley, cinnamon, curry powder and ginger; mix well and simmer for about 10 minutes. Stir in the tomatoes and mix well.

Return the chicken to the pan and turn the pieces to coat them evenly with the pan mixture. Cover the pan and cook over low heat 30 minutes, or until the chicken is tender. Remove the chicken pieces with a slotted spoon to a warm platter, and discard the cinnamon pieces. Stir the peanut butter into the sauce in the pan over medium heat, and when the sauce is thoroughly mixed and thickened, return the chicken to the pan and turn in the sauce to coat thoroughly.

Chicken Trostevere

This dish is named for its originator, Chef Angelo Trostevere of Como, Italy. Chicken legs may be used instead of the chicken cut in serving pieces. Saffron rice is a good choice to serve with it.

Beverly Margolis
Utica, New York

Serves 4 to 6

2½-3 pounds chicken, cut in serving pieces
1 teaspoon salt
¼ teaspoon freshly ground pepper
⅓ cup flour
5 tablespoons olive oil
¼ pound ham, cubed
2 cloves garlic, minced
½ cup dry white wine or dry vermouth
16-ounce can tomatoes
2 green peppers, seeded and cut into rings
1 cup sliced fresh mushrooms
2 medium-size onions, chopped
1 medium-size zucchini, sliced
½ teaspoon dried marjoram
1 tablespoon chopped fresh parsley

Spread the chicken pieces on wax paper and sprinkle them with the salt, pepper and flour. Heat the oil in a skillet and brown the chicken pieces on all sides. Lower the heat and let cook gently 15 to 20 minutes. Remove the chicken from the pan and keep it warm.

Add the ham cubes to the pan and brown them. Remove from the pan and combine with the chicken; keep warm. Add the garlic and wine to the skillet and cook, uncovered, over medium-high heat until the wine is reduced by half. Add the remaining ingredients to the skillet and bring to a boil, stirring to mix well. Reduce heat and simmer 8 to 10 minutes.

Return the chicken and ham cubes to the skillet and simmer all the ingredients together for about 10 minutes longer. Serve hot.

Herb-Stuffed Breasts of Chicken

Mead Brownell
Freeport, Maine

Serves 8
Preheat oven to 350 degrees

4 whole chicken breasts, skinned,
   boned and halved
6 tablespoons butter, at room temperature
1 teaspoon dried thyme
1 tablespoon minced fresh chives
1 teaspoon minced fresh parsley
¼ pound Monterey Jack cheese
½ cup flour
1 egg, lightly beaten
¾ cup breadcrumbs
4 tablespoons grated Parmesan cheese
½ teaspoon ground mace
Salt
Freshly ground pepper
½ cup dry white wine

Remove the fillets from the chicken breasts and reserve for another use. Pound the breast halves between wax paper or plastic wrap until very thin.

Combine the butter, thyme, chive and parsley. Mix well. Divide the Monterey Jack cheese into 8 equal portions. Put 1 portion of cheese and about 1 tablespoon of the herb butter in the center of each breast half, and roll up tightly, tucking in the sides to make a tidy package. Dip each breast in flour to coat lightly.

In a shallow dish combine the egg and 1 tablespoon water. In a second shallow dish, mix with a fork the breadcrumbs, Parmesan, mace, salt and pepper. Dip each floured chicken roll into the egg mixture, then into the crumb mixture, coating well.

Lay them in a buttered ovenproof dish in one layer. If there is any leftover herb butter, it can be melted and sprinkled over.

Bake in the preheated oven 15 minutes. Pour the wine into the baking dish and bake another 35 minutes. Serve hot.

Chicken with Apricots
(Poulet à l'Abricot)

This unusual combination of ingredients makes a fruity but not overly sweet dish. Resist the temptation to cut down on the garlic.

World of Cuisine
Marcia R. Fox
Denver, Colorado

Serves 6
Preheat oven to 350 degrees

2 frying chickens, cut up
½ cup butter
¼ cup peanut oil
1 heaping tablespoon flour
5 large garlic cloves
2 cups apricot liqueur
1 tablespoon lemon juice
1 teaspoon Worcestershire sauce
1 teaspoon salt
Pepper
6 ounces dried apricots

Pat the chicken pieces dry. Combine the butter and oil in a frying pan and sauté the chicken, a few pieces at a time, until golden. Transfer to a large shallow casserole. Pour off about half the fat from the pan. Add the flour to the pan and stir over moderate heat until smoothly blended with the remaining oil. Crush the garlic through a garlic press into the pan and stir it into the flour mixture.

Add the liqueur, lemon juice, Worcestershire sauce and salt and pepper to taste, stirring all together well.

Arrange the apricots in the casserole, tucking them in among the chicken pieces. Pour the sauce over the chicken and apricots. Cover and bake in the preheated oven for 20 minutes. Uncover the casserole and bake a further 20 to 30 minutes, basting occasionally.

Boneless Chicken Breasts with Sour Cream and Chilies

Patricia Tabibian
Wilmington, Delaware

Serves 8 to 10
Preheat oven to 350 degrees

4 tablespoons butter
4 tablespoons vegetable oil
8 whole chicken breasts, boned, skinned and halved

SAUCE:
1½ cloves garlic, peeled
1-2 jalapeño peppers, canned (optional)
1 large onion, roughly chopped
2 cans (4 ounces each) diced green chili peppers
1½ cups sour cream
½ cup milk
2 tablespoons flour
1 teaspoon salt
½ teaspoon white pepper

1 cup shredded sharp cheddar or Monterey Jack cheese
1 teaspoon paprika
Parsley for garnish

Heat half the butter and oil together in a large frying pan. Sauté the chicken pieces quickly on both sides and transfer to a large shallow baking dish, placing them in one layer. Add the rest of the butter and oil to the pan as needed while sautéing.

Combine the sauce ingredients in a food processor with the steel blade. Process until smooth. Spoon the sauce evenly over the chicken, and bake, uncovered, in the preheated oven about 20 minutes. Remove from the oven and sprinkle the cheese on top, then paprika. Return to the oven and bake about 10 minutes longer. To serve, discard any excess fat, and garnish with parsley.

Chicken Thai

Serve with rice.

Rosaleah Goland
Skokie, Illinois

Serves 4 to 6

4 tablespoons vegetable oil
½ cup walnut halves
4 whole chicken breasts, skinned, boned and halved
1 cup coarsely chopped onion
1 clove garlic, minced
1 cup sliced mushrooms
1 cup chopped green pepper
1 teaspoon salt
2 tablespoons brown sugar
1 cup chicken broth
1 tablespoon cornstarch dissolved in
   1 tablespoon cold water

Heat the oil in a deep, heavy skillet. Brown the walnuts, stirring occasionally. Remove and drain.

Add the chicken breast halves to the pan and cook until the meat turns white. Add the onions, garlic, mushrooms, and green pepper, and stir with the chicken. Cook 3 to 5 minutes, stirring frequently.

Mix the salt and brown sugar into the chicken broth and add to the pan. Bring to a boil slowly. Add the cornstarch mixture. Stir until the liquid is thickened and clear. Return the walnuts to the pan. Toss well and serve immediately.

Peppery Chicken with Hot Sauce
(Chicken Chili Relleno with Salsa Cruda)

This dish can be made a day or two ahead; the flavor will improve and it is easily reheated. Pequin are very small peppers.

Creative Cuisinières,
Frazier Farms Cooking School
Kathie Frazier and Amy Wandalowski
Escondido, California

Serves 8 to 10
Preheat oven to 350 degrees

2 tablespoons vegetable oil
2 large onions, chopped
2 cloves garlic, chopped
2 pounds boneless cooked chicken, cut
    into bite-sized pieces
4 crushed dry chili pequin
1 large can green chili peppers,
    drained and seeded
4 cups shredded sharp cheddar cheese
8 eggs
½ cup flour
2 teaspoons salt
¼-½ teaspoon Tabasco sauce

SAUCE:
2 tomatoes, chopped finely
6 scallions, sliced thinly
Few sprigs fresh coriander, loosely chopped
1-2 serrano or jalapeño chili peppers,
    chopped finely
Salt
Freshly ground pepper

Heat the oil in a deep, heavy frying pan and sauté the onion and garlic until limp. Add the chicken and the crushed chili peppers and stir well.

In the bottom of a 9-by-12-inch pan layer half the green chili peppers, then make a layer of 3 cups of the cheese. Spoon on the chicken mixture, and cover with the other half of the green chili peppers.

In a medium-sized bowl, whisk the eggs and flour together. Add the milk, salt and Tabasco and whisk well. Pour over the layered mixture, and sprinkle the remaining cheese on top.

Bake in the preheated oven 45 to 50 minutes.

Meanwhile, make the sauce by combining the tomatoes, scallions, coriander and chili peppers in a bowl, mixing well. Add ⅓ cup of water and salt and pepper to taste.

Remove the baking dish from the oven when the top is well browned. Let stand 5 minutes, then cut in squares and serve with the sauce.

Amaretto Chicken Supreme

Bobbi Saper
Shawnee Mission, Kansas

Serves 4
Preheat oven to 325 degrees

2½-3-pound chicken,
    cut into serving pieces
3 tablespoons flour
1½ teaspoons salt
1½ teaspoons freshly ground white pepper
2 teaspoons paprika
1½ teaspoons garlic salt
1 tablespoon vegetable oil
3 tablespoons butter
1½ tablespoons Dijon mustard
6-ounce can frozen orange juice concentrate,
    thawed, mixed with ½ cup water
1 cup Amaretto liqueur

Rinse the chicken pieces and pat dry. Combine the flour, salt, pepper, paprika and garlic salt, and coat the chicken pieces with the mixture. Heat the oil and butter together in a heavy skillet and sauté the chicken pieces until browned on all sides. Remove the chicken from the skillet and place in an ovenproof casserole, leaving the skillet on low heat.

Add the mustard, orange juice mixture and Amaretto to the skillet. Increase the heat and bring to a boil, stirring constantly, until the sauce has thickened. Pour the sauce over the chicken pieces and bake, covered, in the preheated oven 45 minutes to 1 hour, until the chicken is tender, basting occasionally with the sauce. Serve hot.

Chicken Breasts in Champagne Cream

Here is the perfect answer to the question of what to do with leftover champagne. The bubbles don't matter for this recipe. Fresh asparagus is the best possible accompaniment.

The Von Welanetz Cooking Workshop
Diana Von Welanetz
Pacific Palisades, California

Serves 4 to 6

4 whole chicken breasts, skinned,
   boned and halved
¼ cup all-purpose flour
1 teaspoon salt
½ teaspoon freshly ground white pepper
¾ pound fresh mushrooms
9 tablespoons butter
2 tablespoons vegetable oil
1 cup heavy cream
¼ cup champagne
1 teaspoon lemon juice
1 tablespoon finely chopped parsley

Put the chicken breast halves between two pieces of wax paper or plastic wrap and flatten them slightly with a mallet. Put the flour, salt and pepper in a paper bag and toss the chicken inside the bag. Remove from the bag, shaking off any excess flour mixture.

Clean the mushrooms, discarding the stems, and reserve 8 large ones for garnish. Cut the rest in quarters. Melt 8 tablespoons of the butter and the oil together in a skillet and brown the floured chicken pieces lightly on both sides. Add the mushroom quarters to the pan. Cover, reduce heat and simmer 10 minutes.

Uncover the pan and remove excess butter from the pan with a spoon. Add the cream and champagne and continue to simmer slowly 5 to 7 minutes, uncovered. Remove from heat.

Meanwhile, flute the reserved mushroom caps and sauté them slowly in the remaining tablespoon of butter with the lemon juice sprinkled over them.

To serve, remove the chicken breasts to a warm serving platter. Taste the sauce and add salt and pepper if needed. If it has become too thick, thin it with a little milk or cream. Spoon some sauce over each chicken piece and top with a sautéed mushroom cap. Sprinkle lightly with minced parsley and serve hot.

Pon Pon Chicken

This dish may be served at room temperature,

What's Cooking
Ruth Law
Hinsdale, Illinois

Serves 4

2 large chicken breasts

SAUCE:
2 tablespoons sesame seed paste or
  creamy peanut butter
2 tablespoons sesame oil
2 tablespoons dark soy sauce
1½ tablespoons rice vinegar
1-3 teaspoons hot chili oil
1½ teaspoons sugar
1½ teaspoons finely minced fresh ginger
1½ teaspoons finely minced garlic

⅓ cup raw peanuts
1 cup oil
1 cucumber
⅓ cup shredded scallions

Place the chicken in a saucepan and add water to cover. Bring to a boil and simmer about 15 minutes until the chicken is tender but still firm. Turn off the heat and let the chicken cool in the cooking water. When cool, drain the chicken and tear into strips about 3 inches by ¼ inch.

Make the sauce: Beat the sesame seed paste and sesame oil together in a medium-sized bowl until smooth. Add the soy sauce, vinegar, chili oil — more or less, depending on taste for hot foods — sugar, ginger and garlic. Mix well into a smooth paste.

Deep-fry the peanuts in the oil until golden brown; drain and cool. Place the peanuts between two sheets of waxed paper and crush them with a rolling pin.

Cut the cucumber in half lengthwise and remove the seeds. Slice thinly into half-circle shapes. Arrange in a circle around the edge of a large plate. Inside the circle arrange half of the shredded scallions, and put the chicken strips on top. Pour the sauce over the chicken and sprinkle the peanuts on top. Serve garnished with the rest of the scallions.

Chicken with Mushrooms and Tarragon
(Poulet Princesse)

This recipe is in the style of nouvelle cuisine. Rather than chicken breasts, a cut-up chicken or slices of turkey breast may be substituted, or even cubes of tender beef for a nouvelle version of beef Stroganoff. If preferred, a commercially prepared crème fraîche may be used, or sour cream may be substituted.

Monique Jamet Hooker
Wilmette, Illinois

Serves 4

CRÈME FRAÎCHE:
1½ teaspoons buttermilk or ⅓ cup sour cream
1 cup heavy cream

4 whole chicken breasts, skinned,
   boned and halved
Salt
Freshly ground white pepper
2 tablespoons unsalted butter
2 tablespoons chopped shallots
½ pound mushrooms, sliced
1½ tablespoons fresh tarragon, chopped
1 cup chicken broth, preferably homemade

   Prepare the crème fraîche a day ahead: Combine the ingredients in a jar with a tight screw top. Shake well and leave it at a warm room temperature for 24 hours, or until the mixture has thickened. Shake again and refrigerate.
   Season each chicken breast with salt and pepper. Heat the butter in a heavy skillet and sauté the chicken until golden brown on both sides. Reduce the heat and cook gently for 10 to 15 minutes, until tender. Remove from the pan and keep warm. Pour off any excess fat from the skillet. Add the shallots and sauté briefly. Add the mushrooms and sauté, stirring occasionally, another minute or two. Add 1 tablespoon of the tarragon, stir in over the heat and cook briefly. Pour in the chicken broth and bring to a boil, stirring, to deglaze the pan. Simmer, uncovered, until the sauce is reduced and thickened. Stir in the crème fraîche and simmer for 1 minute. Pour the mixture over the chicken pieces and serve very hot, sprinkled with the remaining fresh tarragon.

Chinese Diced Chicken with Cashews

Constance Quan
Old Greenwich, Connecticut

Serves 4 to 6

MARINADE:
1 egg white
1 tablespoon cornstarch
1 tablespoon light soy sauce
½ teaspoon salt
½ teaspoon sugar

1½ pounds chicken breasts, skinned,
    boned and diced
4 to 6 tablespoons peanut oil
½ cup cashew nuts
½ cup diced sweet red pepper
2 scallions cut in ¼-inch pieces
1 dried hot red pepper, crumbled
2 slices fresh ginger, minced

SAUCE:
½ cup chicken broth
2 tablespoons dry sherry or rice wine
1 tablespoon vinegar
½ teaspoon salt
½ teaspoon sugar
2 teaspoons cornstarch dissolved in
    1 tablespoon cold water

Combine the marinade ingredients in a medium-sized bowl, mixing well with a fork. Toss the chicken pieces in the mixture and set aside to marinate.

Heat 4 tablespoons of the oil in a wok or large shallow frying pan. Stir-fry the cashews for a minute or two over high heat. Remove them with a slotted spoon and place on paper towels or brown paper to drain. Add the chicken to the pan and stir-fry over high heat for a minute or two. Remove with a slotted spoon and keep warm.

If more oil is needed, add 2 tablespoons to the pan and heat. Stir-fry the sweet pepper, scallions, red pepper and ginger until very hot. Add the chicken and toss well. Combine the sauce ingredients, add and cook for about 1 minute longer, stirring and raising the heat if necessary to bring the liquid to a boil. Add the cornstarch mixture and stir over high heat until the mixture is glazed. Serve immediately with the cashews scattered over the top.

Szechuan Duck

Carve this duck at tableside, or you may prefer to chop it in the kitchen into pieces about 2 inches by 4 inches in size, and then reassemble it into the duck shape before serving it on the bed of watercress. Chinese steamed bread and a salt/peppercorn mix may accompany it.

Mary Beth Clark
New York, New York

Serves 4

1 tablespoon Szechuan peppercorns
1 cinnamon stick
1 star anise (8 pods)
2 tablespoons coarse salt
4 slices fresh ginger
1 scallion, cut into pieces and crushed slightly
5- to 6-pound duck, trimmed of excess fat and
   with wing tips removed
2 tablespoons light soy sauce
2 tablespoons flour
2½ teaspoons sesame oil
½ teaspoon sugar
⅛ teaspoon white pepper
6 cups peanut oil
3 cups watercress, stems removed,
   rinsed and dried

Roast the peppercorns, cinnamon, anise and salt in a hot oven or in a heavy skillet over heat until the salt is slightly browned and the spices are fragrant. Crush slightly. Rub the ginger and scallion pieces over the inner surfaces of the duck along with half the spice mixture. Leave inside the cavity. Rub the other half of the spice mixture over the outside of the duck. Wrap the duck in foil and refrigerate for 24 hours.

Remove the ginger and scallions from inside the duck and discard. Place the duck in a steaming rack over boiling water and steam, with the entire container covered, for 1½ hours. As soon as it is cool enough to handle, rub the outside of the duck with half of the soy sauce, and let dry thoroughly. Rub the outside of the duck with flour and let stand for 10 minutes. Combine the remaining soy sauce with the sesame oil, sugar and pepper, and toss with the watercress. Arrange the watercress on a serving platter.

Heat the peanut oil to 350 degrees in a deep fryer and fry the duck, turning it until it is golden brown, about 7 minutes on each side. Drain well before carving. Serve the pieces on a bed of watercress.

Braised Duck with Rice
(Rizses Kacsa)

This Hungarian dish should be served with
Hungarian wine, and a crisp green salad.

Judith Goldinger
Schererville, Indiana

Serves 6 to 8
Preheat oven to 375 degrees

1 large duck, boned and cut into 1-inch cubes
5 tablespoons rendered fat from the duck
1 large onion, chopped
2 carrots, sliced
2 stalks celery, sliced
2 parsnips, sliced
Salt
Freshly ground pepper
½ teaspoon dried marjoram
¼-½ cup broth made from the duck bones
   and giblets, or chicken broth
½ pound mushrooms, sliced
1 cup long-grain rice
¼ pound shelled peas or 10-ounce package
   frozen peas, thawed
¼ cup chopped parsley
Hungarian paprika

Brown the duck pieces in 2 tablespoons of the
rendered duck fat in a heavy skillet that has a
cover. Add the onion and cook gently, taking care
not to let it brown. Add the carrots, celery,
parsnips, salt, pepper and marjoram. Cook, stirring
frequently, for about 5 minutes. Add ¼ cup of the
broth; bring to a boil, lower the heat, cover the pan
and simmer gently about 30 minutes, checking
from time to time and adding water or more broth
if needed.

Meanwhile, in a heavy flameproof casserole,
sauté the mushrooms in 2 tablespoons of the
rendered duck fat. Add the rice and stir over heat
until the rice becomes opaque. Add the peas and
most of the parsley, and season with salt and
pepper. Remove from the heat.

Take the skillet off the heat and skim as much
fat as possible from the surface, leaving the pan
juices. Add the contents of the skillet to the
casserole and add 2 cups of water. Return to the
heat and bring to a boil. Cover tightly and transfer
to the preheated oven. Bake 25 to 30 minutes.

While the dish is baking, put the remaining
tablespoon of duck fat into the skillet and sauté
the duck liver until golden brown, sprinkling with
paprika as it cooks. Slice the liver and keep warm.

To serve the casserole, scatter the liver slices on
top. Garnish with more paprika and the remaining
chopped parsley.

Quail with Grapes
(Cailles Flambées aux Raisins)

L'Academie de Cuisine
François Dionot
Bethesda, Maryland

Serves 4
Preheat oven to 400 degrees

8 quails
Salt
Freshly ground black pepper
1 pound seedless grapes
4 apples
2 tablespoons vegetable oil
8 tablespoons butter
Pinch of grated nutmeg
⅓ cup champagne or Calvados

Clean the quails. Reserve the giblets and season inside and out with salt and pepper. Reserve 1 cup of the grapes. Stuff the quails with the remaining grapes.

Cut each apple in half. Core them and slice off a small piece from the bottom of each half so it sits firmly without rolling. Place in a buttered baking dish.

Heat the oil and 2 tablespoons of the butter in a large, heavy, ovenproof skillet that can accommodate all the quails at once. Sauté them, turning often to color evenly. Add the quails' kidneys, livers and hearts to the skillet and place in the preheated oven. Bake 15 minutes, basting frequently. Bake the apple halves at the same time.

Remove the grapes from the quails; put them in the skillet and crush lightly. Set over low heat to cook gently 5 minutes. Put the quails in a warm oven, covered with foil. Put the apples in the same oven.

Press the grape mixture from the pan through a fine sieve, and return to the pan after discarding the skins. Bring to a boil and cook uncovered until reduced by half. Add nutmeg and remove from heat. Stir in 4 tablespoons butter.

In another pan, heat the remaining 2 tablespoons butter and sauté the reserved grapes for 1 minute. To serve, top each apple half with a sautéed quail and arrange around a large warm platter. Heat the champagne or Calvados and pour into a small heated sauceboat. Place this in the center of the platter and scatter the sautéed grapes around the edges. At the table, set the spirits alight and pour over the quails while still flaming.

Rolled Baked Stuffed Eggplant

Marie Agresti
Franklin Square, New York

Serves 5 to 6
Preheat the broiler; then preheat
   the oven to 350 degrees

1 long eggplant, about 1 pound
3 eggs, lightly beaten
¼ teaspoon salt
1 teaspoon milk
1½ cups dry breadcrumbs, preferably the
   Italian seasoned type
¾ cup olive oil

FILLING:
1 egg, lightly beaten
2 cups ricotta cheese
½ pound mozzarella cheese, grated
¼ cup grated romano cheese

SAUCE:
2 tablespoons olive oil
1 medium-size onion, finely chopped
2 cloves garlic, finely chopped
28-ounce can Italian plum tomatoes,
   drained, chopped and pressed through
   a sieve
1 large can tomato puree
1 tablespoon finely chopped parsley,
   preferably the Italian type
2 leaves fresh basil or 1 teaspoon dried basil
1 tablespoon grated romano cheese
2 tablespoons port wine
⅛ teaspoon grated nutmeg
1 bay leaf
Cayenne pepper
Salt

Peel the eggplant and cut it lengthwise in slices ¼ inch thick. Combine the eggs with the salt and milk in a shallow dipping dish. Combine the eggs in a second dipping dish, and the oil in a third. Dip the eggplant slices first in the egg mixture and then into the crumbs, coating both sides well. Then dip, one side only, in the oil, and place in a large shallow baking pan, oiled side up, in one layer only. Broil on the level closest to the heat, until brown on the top side. Turn the eggplant slices over and brown the other side. Transfer to wax paper when browned.

Make the filling: Combine the egg and ricotta. Mix well. Add the mozzarella and romano. Mix well. Spread about 2 tablespoons of the cheese mixture on each slice of eggplant, and roll the eggplant up to enclose the filling, starting with the narrow end. Place the eggplant rolls, seams down, in one layer in a baking dish.

Make the sauce: Heat the olive oil in a heavy saucepan and sauté the onion and garlic until soft. Add the tomatoes and tomato puree, and bring to a boil, stirring. Add the remaining sauce ingredients, stir well and bring to a boil again. Lower the heat and simmer, uncovered, for half an hour, stirring occasionally. Remove the bay leaf and pour the sauce over the eggplant rolls in the baking dish. Bake, uncovered, in the preheated oven for 20 minutes. Uncover the pan and bake another 25 minutes. Serve hot.

Vegetable Lasagne

This can be made with any firm pasta, such as shells or fusilli, in place of lasagna, if preferred.

Marla Horn
Hollywood, Florida

Serves 6
Preheat oven to 350 degrees

2 pounds ricotta or cottage cheese
1 cup freshly grated romano or Parmesan cheese
1 cup coarsely grated mozzarella cheese
1 cup coarsely grated Swiss or Edam cheese
3 eggs, lightly beaten
2 medium-size zucchini, cut in
    ¼-inch slices
1 small bunch broccoli, florets only
3 tablespoons butter
3 tablespoons olive oil
4 cloves garlic, coarsely chopped
4 medium-size onions, coarsely chopped
28-ounce can Italian plum tomatoes in puree
¼ teaspoon dried oregano
¼ teaspoon dried basil
Salt
Freshly ground pepper
1 pound lasagne
Additional grated cheese (optional)

Combine all four cheeses with the eggs in a large bowl. Mix well.

Steam the zucchini for 2 minutes. Drain and reserve. Steam the broccoli florets for 5 minutes. Drain and reserve.

Heat the butter and olive oil in a large skillet and sauté the garlic and onions until tender. Add the tomatoes and their puree. Stir to break them up, and cook over medium heat until the sauce has thickened. Add the oregano and basil, and salt and pepper to taste.

Cook the lasagne in boiling salted water until done *al dente.* Drain well.

Oil a lasagne pan and spread sauce on the bottom. Add a layer of lasagne, then a layer of zucchini, a layer of broccoli, and a layer of the cheese mixture. Repeat the layers and top with sauce. Sprinkle additional grated cheese on top, if desired, and bake in the preheated oven for 35 minutes, or until bubbly. Serve at once.

Broiled Swordfish Steaks

A good rule of thumb for broiling swordfish is ten minutes per inch of thickness.

Marlene Parrish Teaches Cooking!
Marlene Parrish
Sewickley, Pennsylvania

Serves 4
Preheat the broiler

4 swordfish steaks, about 1 inch thick
MARINADE:
½ cup soy sauce
½ cup olive oil
½ cup dry sherry
2 garlic cloves, finely chopped
2 tablespoons finely chopped fresh ginger
2 tablespoons grated zest of orange

Cherry tomatoes for garnish
Lime wedges for garnish

Place the fish in a shallow dish. Combine the marinade ingredients and pour over the fish. Leave to marinate for about an hour, turning the fish and basting occasionally.

Remove the fish to an oiled rack in a broiler pan. Reserve the marinade. Broil about 4 inches from the heat for about 6 minutes, then turn the fish over and broil about 4 minutes more. Baste frequently with the marinade during broiling.

Transfer the fish to a heated serving platter. With the broiler pan over heat, add the remaining marinade. Heat quickly and pour over the fish, or into a sauceboat. Serve the fish garnished with cherry tomatoes and lime wedges.

Scallops of Salmon with Sorrel-Cream Sauce
(Escalopes de Saumon à l'Oselle)

David Robert Berger
Washington, D.C.

Serves 8

1 bunch fresh sorrel leaves
4 salmon fillets, about ¾ pound each, cut from tail end
4-6 tablespoons clarified butter
4 shallots, finely chopped
1 bottle dry white wine
1¼ cups heavy cream
Coarse salt
Freshly ground white pepper

Prepare a "chiffonade" of the sorrel leaves: Remove the stems and any discolored leaves. Wash and dry well, and shred the leaves into thin strips.

Place the fillets, one at a time, between two pieces of wax paper, and flatten slightly. Cut each flattened fillet in half.

Heat the clarified butter in a large heavy skillet and sauté the scallops of salmon lightly. As soon as cooked, set aside and keep warm. Add the shallots to the skillet and sauté lightly, 1 to 2 minutes. Add the wine and cook over high heat uncovered, until it is reduced by two-thirds. Stir in the cream and cook over medium-high heat until a light-sauce consistency. Season to taste with salt and pepper. Fold in the chiffonade of sorrel leaves and serve immediately over the salmon.

Whole Stuffed Baked Fish

The quantities of the vegetables used to stuff the fish in this recipe may be doubled, if desired, to provide a bed of vegetables under the fish during baking, then to be served as a side dish.

Bailee Kronowitz
Savannah, Georgia

Serves 6 to 8
Preheat oven to 375 degrees

1 trout or bass, about 5 pounds
1 teaspoon dried thyme
1 teaspoon dried tarragon
1 teaspoon dried basil
1 teaspoon garlic powder
1 teaspoon salt
1 teaspoon freshly ground black pepper
1 medium-size onion, coarsely chopped
2 large carrots, coarsely chopped
2 stalks celery, chopped
3 cloves garlic, crushed
Juice of 2 lemons
1 to 2 tablespoons Worcestershire sauce
3 tablespoons butter
Lemon slices for garnish

Gut and scale the fish. Leave head and tail intact. Rinse the fish well, inside and out, to remove all loose scales and any blood. Slit the underside of the fish up to the bone.

Combine the thyme, tarragon, basil, garlic powder, salt and pepper. Rub the mixture onto the inner and outer surfaces of the fish.

Combine the onion, carrots, celery and garlic. Stuff the cavity of the fish with the mixture. Sew up the bottom of the fish, then form the stuffed fish into a circle and sew the head to the tail securely. Place the fish in the bottom of a baking pan and scatter in any extra vegetable mixture.

Mix the lemon juice with Worcestershire sauce to taste, and pour the mixture over the fish. Dot the top with butter, and bake in the preheated oven about 30 minutes, or until the fish is done (test by putting a fork in the underside of the fish; if it twists easily, it is ready). Remove all sewing threads. Serve hot, surrounded by vegetables and lemon slices.

Poached Fish à la Parisienne

This dish can also be made satisfactorily with any firm-fleshed white fish, or with scallops in place of fish.

Joan Polin
Melrose Park, Pennsylvania

Serves 4 to 6
Preheat oven to 350 degrees

1½ pounds cod
1 onion, sliced
1 shallot, sliced
Salt
Pepper
1½ cups dry white wine, or enough to cover the fish
1 bouquet garni (½ teaspoon dried thyme, 1 bay leaf and 3 sprigs parsley tied in cheesecloth)
6 tablespoons butter
½ pound fresh mushrooms, sliced
2 tablespoons flour
½ cup heavy cream
⅓ cup dry breadcrumbs
¾ cup grated Swiss cheese

Lay the fish in a shallow skillet and cover with the onion and the shallot. Season with salt and pepper. Add the wine and the bouquet garni and bring slowly to a boil. Lower the heat, cover the pan and simmer 15 to 20 minutes, or until the fish flakes easily.

Meanwhile, heat 2 tablespoons of the butter in a small skillet and sauté the mushrooms for about 3 minutes. Set aside.

When the fish is cooked, remove it from the skillet and let it cool slightly. Pour the pan juices from the fish skillet into a strainer, spooning in the onions and shallots as well. Press through the strainer and reserve. Flake the fish, removing the bones.

In a heavy saucepan, heat the remaining butter. Reserve half of it in a warm place. Add the flour to the saucepan and cook, stirring, to make a roux. Add the reserved pan juices and cook, whisking constantly, until the sauce has thickened slightly. Gradually stir in the cream. Cook gently until it becomes thick again. Adjust the seasonings.

In the bottom of a 2-quart casserole, spread a thin layer of the sauce, then spoon the flaked fish on top, then add a layer of mushrooms and finally a layer of the remaining sauce. Sprinkle the breadcrumbs and grated cheese on top and spoon the reserved melted butter over them. Bake in the preheated oven 20 minutes, or until the sauce bubbles. Serve very hot.

Gingered Scallops

Richard Nelson Cooking Classes
Richard Nelson
Portland, Oregon

Serves 6

6 tablespoons butter
2 tablespoons finely chopped fresh ginger
1½ pounds bay scallops
Salt
Freshly ground white pepper
2 tablespoons finely chopped parsley for garnish

Heat the butter in a large skillet until it sizzles. Sauté the ginger briefly. Add the scallops and sauté just until the scallops are heated through. They will turn opaque. Season to taste with salt and pepper. Garnish with parsley and serve at once.

Shrimp with Feta Cheese and Pasta

Jill Heavenrich
Milwaukee, Wisconsin

Serves 8 to 10
Preheat oven to 400 degrees

2 pounds large uncooked shrimp,
    peeled and deveined
1 tablespoon lemon juice
¼ cup olive oil
¾ cup finely chopped shallots
1½ cups canned Italian plum tomatoes,
    drained and coarsely chopped
2 cloves garlic
Salt
Freshly ground pepper
½ cup clam juice
1 teaspoon dried oregano
½ cup dry white wine
½ pound feta cheese, drained of
    brine if necessary
3 tablespoons butter
1 pound spaghetti

Pat the shrimp with paper towels and put in a shallow bowl. Sprinkle with the lemon juice.

Heat the olive oil in a heavy saucepan that has a cover and sauté the shallots until soft and opaque. Add the chopped tomatoes, the garlic, forced through a garlic press, and salt and pepper to taste. Bring to a boil, stirring. Lower the heat and simmer very slowly, covered, for 20 minutes. Add the clam juice and stir in . Simmer 5 minutes longer. Taste and adjust seasonings.

Pour the sauce into a shallow baking dish and lay the raw shrimp on top of the sauce. Sprinkle with oregano and pour in the wine, distributing it evenly throughout the dish. Crumble the feta cheese over the surface. Bake, uncovered, in the preheated oven for 15 minutes.

Put the butter in a large ovenproof serving dish and place it in the oven for a few moments, only long enough for the butter to melt. Keep the dish warm.

Bring a large quantity of salted water to a boil in a pan that has a lid. Add the spaghetti, stirring to separate. Bring to a second rolling boil and cook fast for 2 minutes. Remove the pan from the heat, cover with a towel and then the lid. Let stand for about 8 minutes, then test. If "al dente," pour immediately into a large colander to drain. Shake the colander well to remove all moisture, then transfer the noodles to the warm serving dish and immediately toss well to combine with the melted butter. Spoon the shrimp mixture onto the pasta and serve immediately.

Squid with Tomato Sauce
(Calamari con Salsa Pomodoro)

This is a good sauce to serve with any plain pasta. It may be prepared ahead of time: omit the final simmering until just before serving time. If fresh squid is not available, it can be made with frozen squid, well thawed.

Nell Benedict
Lathrup Village, Michigan

Serves 4

3-5 pounds fresh squid
½ cup Frascati or other dry white wine
1 bay leaf
3 sprigs parsley
2 cloves garlic
¼ teaspoon dried thyme
1 teaspoon salt
5 black peppercorns

SAUCE:
2 tablespoons vegetable oil
3 cloves garlic, finely chopped
1 small onion, finely chopped
1 small carrot, finely chopped
28-ounce can tomato sauce
¼ cup dry red wine
1 teaspoon dried oregano
1 teaspoon dried basil
1 tablespoon finely minced parsley
1 teaspoon, or more, salt
¼ teaspoon freshly ground pepper

Clean the squid: Grasp each squid firmly by the tail and pull the tail away from the head and tentacles. Find the mouth, which is hidden in the center of the tentacles, and discard it. Holding the squid under running water, peel off the thin outer skin. Discard. Squeeze out and discard all the insides, including a transparent center bone. Wash well under running water, then place in a saucepan. Add the wine, bay leaf, parsley, garlic, thyme, salt and peppercorns, and water to cover. Bring to a boil, lower the heat, cover and simmer for 40 minutes.

As soon as the squid is simmering, prepare the sauce: Heat the oil in a large saucepan and sauté the garlic, onion and carrot until softened. Add the remaining sauce ingredients, stir well and simmer, partly covered, for 30 minutes, or until the sauce has thickened, stirring often to avoid scorching.

While the sauce is still cooking, drain the squid and discard the cooking liquid. Rinse the squid well under running water and cut them into rings ¼ inch thick. Add them to the simmering sauce. Continue to simmer just long enough to heat the squid through. Taste and adjust seasonings. Serve over the hot pasta.

Vegetable Accompaniments

In the hands of an imaginative cook, vegetables can be elevated from the ordinary to the exceptional. And as the number of imaginative cooks among us increases, so do the variety and quality of vegetables presented in local produce sections and at greengrocers. Only a few years ago, eggplant and artichokes, for example, were rarely seen in most markets. But these days, these and many other once-unfamiliar foods regularly contribute to the spectrum of fresh vegetable choices available almost everywhere.

Vegetables often "marry" well — a classic case of this is ratatouille — but many well-prepared vegetable dishes are worthy to stand alone, and may be served in place of a salad or first course or in addition to these.

Today the art of vegetable and salad preparation is in its prime, catered to creatively in magazine and newspaper features, but seldom as variously as in this chapter. Give them respect and attention in the preparation, and vegetables will always reward your efforts to please and nourish those who come to your table.

Stuffed Artichoke Hearts

Any leftover stuffing made for this dish may be frozen and will make a good filling for stuffed mushrooms on another occasion.

Charlotte Ann Albertson's
*   Kitchen Saucer Cooking School*
Charlotte Ann Albertson
Wynnewood, Pennsylvania

Serves 6
Preheat oven to 400 degrees

2 cans (14 ounces each) artichoke hearts
STUFFING:
1 cup fresh breadcrumbs
2 tablespoons grated Parmesan cheese
½ cup olive oil, or anchovy or sardine oil
1 tablespoon chopped parsley
1 tablespoon oregano
1 clove garlic, minced
Salt
Pepper

2 tablespoons unsalted butter
Pimiento or julienned red pepper to garnish

Drain and rinse the artichoke hearts. Cut each bottom flat to form a level base. With finger or thumb, gently enlarge the cavity in the center of each artichoke heart.

Mix all the stuffing ingredients thoroughly, and stuff the hearts with the mixture, mounding it generously. Place in an oiled baking dish and top each one with a little butter.

At this stage they may be refrigerated to be baked later, or baked at once.

Bake in the preheated oven for 15 to 20 minutes. Serve warm or cold, garnished with pimiento or red pepper.

Onion Flowers with Pecans

Nathalie Dupree
Atlanta, Georgia

Serves 4
Preheat oven to 250 degrees

4 large Vidalia or Bermuda onions
Salt
4 teaspoons red wine vinegar
¾ cup peanut oil
½ cup coarsely chopped pecan halves
Freshly ground pepper
4 tablespoons lemon juice
2 tablespoons chopped parsley

The day before serving, peel the onions, leaving the roots trimmed but intact. Cut each from the top down, not cutting through the root end, in slices about ¼ inch apart at the fattest part of the onion. Turn the onion at right angles and cut again so that when placed standing on its root end the onion will form a chrysanthemum design. Ignore any loose onion sections in the middle.

Salt the onions and place on root ends in a lightly oiled baking dish. Spoon the vinegar and about half the oil over them until each is well coated. Cover the pan lightly with foil and bake in the preheated oven for 2 hours, basting several times. Add a few chopped pecans to the center of each onion, and bake for another hour.

Remove from the oven and sprinkle pepper, oil and lemon juice over the onions. Garnish with parsley and refrigerate overnight. Serve cool or at room temperature.

Turkish Stuffed Eggplant
(Imam Bayildi)

The name of this famous Turkish vegetable dish translates roughly as "the priest fainted," but opinions vary as to why — whether he was overcome by the sublime aroma and taste of the dish, or at the prodigious quantity of olive oil, for which he was to pay the bill. Yogurt is good with this.

L'Epicure School of Cooking
Rosa Rajkovic
Albuquerque, New Mexico

Serves 6
Preheat oven to 350 degrees

3 medium-size long, firm eggplants
Salt
¾ cup olive oil
3 medium-size onions, sliced
4 cloves garlic, minced
6 large tomatoes, peeled and coarsely chopped
⅝ cup chopped parsley
¼ teaspoon cinnamon
1 teaspoon sugar

Freshly ground pepper
Wedges of tomato and lemon for garnish

Cut off the ends of the eggplants, and cut strips off the skin lengthwise with a potato peeler. Cut the eggplants in half lengthwise. Scoop out about a third of the pulp from each half and put in a chopping bowl. Chop coarsely. Sprinkle the eggplant shells generously with salt to drain off the bitter juices, and turn them face down on paper towels. Sprinkle the pulp with salt and transfer to paper towels to drain. Leave for about 45 minutes.

Gently squeeze the eggplant shells and the pulp to extract any additional juices, then rinse the salt off and squeeze again. Pat dry.

Heat ½ cup of the olive oil and sauté the onions until golden. Add the garlic and sauté for 1 to 2 minutes. Add the chopped eggplant pulp. Sauté the mixture 4 to 5 minutes. Add the tomatoes, ½ cup of the parsley, the cinnamon and sugar. Simmer 30 minutes. Add salt and pepper to taste.

Arrange the eggplant shells side by side, face up, in a large oiled baking pan, and divide the onion and tomato mixture among them, mounding it neatly. Cover the pan with foil and bake in the preheated oven for about 1 hour, until the eggplant is soft. Drizzle more olive oil over the baked eggplant and serve, garnished with the remaining chopped parsley and wedges of lemon and tomato.

Braised Cucumbers

The virtuous cucumber remains low in calories even when cooked. If preferred, rather than being sliced they may be cut in chunks and seeded before cooking.

Judith Bell
Chicago, Illinois

Serves 4

1 chicken bouillon cube dissolved
　in ⅓ cup water
3 medium-size cucumbers, peeled and sliced
　on the bias
1 teaspoon dill weed, or ½ teaspoon
　curry powder

Bring the ⅓ cup bouillon mixture to a boil in a medium-sized skillet or saucepan. Add the cucumbers and dill weed or curry powder, and cook briefly, only until the cucumber is tender. Remove with a slotted spoon and serve at once.

Beets Dijon

This is an unusual and tasty, but very easy, dish to make.

Modern Gourmet of Milwaukee
Myra Dorros
Milwaukee, Wisconsin

Serves 6

4 large beets
3 tablespoons unsalted butter
¼ cup cognac
½ cup heavy cream
4 tablespoons grainy-style Dijon mustard
Salt
Pepper

Peel the beets and cut in julienne strips. Heat the butter in a skillet and sauté the beet strips until tender. Remove from the pan.

Turning the heat to high, add the cognac to the skillet and stir any brown bits from the bottom of the pan. Add the cream and mustard, and cook, still over high heat, until the mixture has reduced by half, stirring continuously. Return the beets to the pan and toss, adding salt and pepper to taste. Serve hot.

Spinach with Vinegar, Garlic and Pine Nuts

(Spinacci con Aceto, Aglio e Pinolli)

Sharon W. Lane
Irvine, California

Serves 4

2 pounds fresh spinach, well cleaned
¼ cup olive oil
2 cloves garlic, crushed
2 tablespoons vinegar
4 tablespoons pine nuts

Put the spinach in a pan with just enough boiling salted water to cover the bottom of the pan. Cook until limp. Drain and refresh under cold running water. Drain again and press out all excess moisture.

Heat the oil in a frying pan and sauté the garlic until golden. Add the spinach and sauté until the spinach is almost dry. Add the vinegar and toss well. Garnish with the pine nuts, and serve.

Sautéed Green Beans

(Haricots Verts)

Select beans of approximately equal lengths, if possible, for this dish.

Ruth H. Howse
Memphis, Tennessee

Serves 4

1 pound green beans
Salt
2 tablespoons butter
Freshly ground pepper

Wash the beans and cut off the ends. Drop into 2 quarts of boiling salted water and cook about 8 minutes, until cooked but still crunchy. Drain and rinse briefly under cold water to stop the cooking process. Spread on paper towels to dry.

Heat the butter in a skillet and add the beans, salt and pepper. Sauté, tossing, until the beans are lightly browned, and serve at once.

Strata Potatoes

To serve more than six people, double this recipe and bake in two separate pans, rather than simply increasing amounts, or the potatoes will not cook properly.

Carol's Cuisine
Carol Giudice
Staten Island, New York

Serves 5 to 6
Preheat oven to 350 degrees

4-6 tablespoons butter
5 Idaho potatoes, sliced as thinly as possible
2 ripe tomatoes, sliced
½ Bermuda onion, sliced
1 to 2 green peppers, sliced
⅛ teaspoon marjoram
1 clove garlic, minced
Salt
Pepper
½ cup chicken broth
½ teaspoon paprika

Butter a 9-by-13-by-2-inch baking dish and layer in the vegetables, first half of the potato slices, then all the tomatoes, then all the onions, then all the peppers. Sprinkle with marjoram, garlic, salt and pepper, and dot with butter. Top with a layer of the remaining potato slices. Pour the chicken broth over the potatoes and dot with butter again. Bake in the preheated oven for half an hour, then gently turn the contents of the baking dish to mix the vegetables. If the dish seems to be too dry, add more chicken broth. Bake for another half hour and turn again. The potatoes should be well done. If not, bake another half hour.

When done, sprinkle lightly with paprika, dot with more butter and slide under the broiler to brown.

Missouri Baked Tomatoes

Pampered Pantry
Marie Mosher
St. Louis, Missouri

Serves 6 to 8
Preheat oven to 300 degrees

8 slices bread, generously buttered
3 pounds ripe tomatoes, peeled and sliced
   (about 11 tomatoes)
Salt
Pepper
1 medium-size onion, finely chopped
1 clove garlic, minced
1 handful fresh basil leaves, chopped
Several sprigs fresh parsley, minced
⅔ cup light brown sugar
1 to 2 tablespoons butter

   Toast the bread in the preheated oven until dry and crisp. Break into bite-sized pieces.
   Butter a 2-quart baking dish and arrange a layer of tomatoes in the bottom. Season with salt and pepper and add about a third each of the onion, garlic, basil, parsley, toasted bread and brown sugar. Repeat, forming two more layers, ending with a generous topping of toast and brown sugar.
   Bake in the preheated oven 3 to 4 hours, until thick and "candied." The edges should be brown and crisp when done. Dot with butter immediately upon taking from the oven. Turn off the heat and replace in the oven for a moment or two before serving.

Mushrooms Florentine

Judith Martin
Port Huron, Michigan

Serves 6 to 8
Preheat oven to 350 degrees

2 tablespoons butter
1 pound fresh mushrooms, sliced
¼ cup chopped onion
1 clove garlic, minced
1 pound fresh spinach, or 2 (10-ounce)
   packages frozen spinach, cooked,
   drained and chopped
1 teaspoon salt
¼ cup melted butter
2 cups grated Muenster cheese

Heat the butter in a skillet and sauté the mushrooms until tender. Remove from the pan and reserve. Add the onion and garlic to the pan and sauté until the onion is tender but not brown.
   Put the spinach, salt and melted butter in a bowl. Add the onion and garlic and mix well. Spoon the mixture into a 1½-quart baking dish and press down gently to firm. Sprinkle half the cheese over the top, spoon the sautéed mushrooms over it and cover with the remaining cheese. Bake in the preheated oven for about 20 minutes, until the cheese is lightly browned and bubbly.

Bulgur with Mushrooms
(Duxelles Bulgur)

A staple in the Middle East, bulgur is cracked wheat that has been parboiled and dried. In America it can be purchased at many markets and specialty food shops.

Cordon Rose
Rose Levy Beranbaum
New York, New York

Serves 4

4 tablespoons butter
4 cups mushrooms, finely chopped
1 clove garlic, crushed
1 cup fine bulgur
¼ teaspoon sugar
1 teaspoon salt
¼ teaspoon pepper

Heat the butter in a large skillet and add the mushrooms and garlic. Cook gently, covered, but stirring occasionally, for about an hour, until the mushrooms turn brown and all the liquid they have released has evaporated. Remove the garlic. Add the bulgur and stir in with a fork. Cook for a few minutes, until the bulgur browns slightly. Add the sugar, salt and pepper, and 1½ cups of salted boiling water. Do not stir. Simmer, covered, about 15 minutes, until the bulgur is dry and tender. Remove from the heat and stir with a fork. Cover and let stand for 5 to 10 minutes before serving.

Onion Casserole

Onions are wonderfully versatile and plentiful. This casserole can be served hot as a vegetable side dish or chilled and accompanied by a vinaigrette sauce. Make the sauce of one quarter wine vinegar, three quarters oil and several fresh herbs, preferably parsley, tarragon, chives and chervil. Cold, this makes a fine picnic dish; take the vinaigrette along in a flask. And don't forget the salt and pepper.

Richard Nelson Cooking Classes
Richard Nelson
Portland, Oregon

Serves 8
Preheat oven to 325 degrees

7-8 cups chopped onion
4 tablespoons butter
½ cup rice
1 cup grated Swiss cheese
⅔ cup half-and-half
1 teaspoon salt

Sauté the onions in the butter until transparent. Cook the rice in 5 cups of boiling water for 5 minutes. Drain and mix with the onions. Add the cheese and half-and-half. Mix well and place in a buttered baking dish. Bake in the preheated oven, uncovered, for 1 hour.

Vegetable Marengo

A see-through baking dish is likely to prove convenient in cooking this dish.

Hilltop Herb Farm Cooking School
Gwen Barclay and Madalene Hill
Cleveland, Texas

Serves 6 to 8
Preheat oven to 350 degrees

4 to 6 tablespoons butter
4 medium-size new potatoes, skin on,
   scrub-brushed and cut in ¼-inch slices
1 tablespoon finely chopped fresh sage
1 tablespoon fresh tarragon
Salt
3 green peppers, cut in ¼-inch cubes
1 medium-size onion, cut in ¼-inch slices
½ cup uncooked rice
3 medium-size zucchini, cut in ¼-inch slices
4 medium-size ripe tomatoes, cut in thick slices
1 cup grated cheddar cheese

Butter a 2½-quart baking dish or casserole. Lay half the potato slices in the bottom. Dot with a little of the butter and sprinkle with a pinch of the sage, a little tarragon and salt. Add a layer of half the green pepper, then a layer of half the onion. Over that, sprinkle half the rice. Dot the butter, add sage, tarragon and salt. Then a layer of half the zucchini and a layer of half the tomatoes. Again dot with butter, and add sage, tarragon and salt.

Repeat the entire process: first the potatoes, butter and seasonings, then peppers, onions and rice, butter and seasonings, zucchini and tomato, butter and seasonings.

Press down on the top layer so the vegetables are not above the top of the baking dish and cover tightly with foil. Bake in the preheated oven 1 hour. Remove from the oven and take off the foil to see if the potatoes are done. If not, bake another 30 minutes, increasing the oven temperature if there is too much liquid remaining.

When the potatoes are done, remove from the oven, take off the foil and sprinkle the cheese over the top. Put back in the oven long enough for the cheese to melt. Let rest, covered, for 10 minutes before serving.

Spinach Balls Parmesan

Here are iron and Vitamin A in a form even
children will love.

Gourmet Stop!
Laura Lempert
Houston, Texas

Serves 8

3 tablespoons butter
3 cups freshly-cooked spinach,
  chopped and drained
2 eggs
1½ cups breadcrumbs
½ cup grated Parmesan cheese
3 tablespoons grated onion
¼ teaspoon salt
Pepper
3 cups vegetable oil

    Put the butter in a warm bowl and add the hot
freshly cooked spinach. Mix well. Add 1 egg, ½
cup breadcrumbs, 3 tablespoons of the Parmesan
cheese and all the grated onion, and mix well. Add
salt and pepper. Cool the mixture, then form into
balls 1½ inches in diameter.
    Combine the other egg with 2 tablespoons water
in a small dipping dish and mix with a fork. In a
second dipping dish, mix the remaining breadcrumbs and Parmesan.
    Heat the vegetable oil in a deep fryer to
375 degrees.
    Roll the spinach balls first in the egg mixture,
then in the crumb mixture, and fry in deep fat
about 10 minutes. Drain and serve at once.

Ratatouille with Turnips
(Ratatouille des Navets)

Cinnamon Toast
Yvonne Moody and Lois Lee
Minnetonka, Minnesota

Serves 6 to 8
Preheat oven to 425 degrees

2 tablespoons vegetable or olive oil
1 leek, sliced and washed carefully
1 medium-size onion, peeled and sliced
1 small green pepper, sliced
1 clove garlic, minced
6 turnips, peeled and sliced
Salt
Pepper
2 tomatoes, peeled and chopped
⅛ teaspoon dried basil
½ cup grated Swiss cheese

    Heat the oil in a heavy pan that has a lid, and
sauté the leek, onion, green pepper and garlic 2 to
3 minutes. Stir in the turnips, salt and pepper, and
sauté another minute or two. Stir in the tomatoes
and basil. Cover and cook over low heat for about
20 minutes.
    Spread the mixture in a gratin dish and scatter
the Swiss cheese over the top. About 15 minutes
before serving, put the dish in the preheated oven
to get very hot, so it can be served with the cheese
nicely melted.

Tomatoes Carnelian

Sharon Baird
Edina, Minnesota

Serves 8
Preheat oven to 375 degrees

8 tablespoons butter
1 small onion, finely chopped
½ pound mushrooms, finely chopped
¼ cup finely chopped fresh parsley
Salt
Pepper
½ cup fresh breadcrumbs
2 teaspoons Dijon mustard
4 tomatoes, cores and stems removed,
    cut in half

Heat the butter in a skillet over medium to high heat. Add the onion and sauté until wilted. Add the mushrooms and parsley and cook gently until the excess liquid has evaporated, still over fairly high heat. Remove from the heat and stir in the salt, pepper, breadcrumbs and mustard.

Mound the mixture on top of the tomato halves, pressing it gently and smoothing it into a firm shape. At this point, the tomatoes may either be refrigerated, covered, for up to 24 hours, or they may be baked at once.

Put the tomato halves in a buttered gratin dish and bake in the preheated oven for 15 to 20 minutes, or until well heated through.

Spicy Potato Shreds with Scallions

This recipe is given as it was served at The People's Hotel in Xuan, China in July 1979. The thinly shredded potato is quickly stir-fried, and when eaten hot is still slightly crisp. It goes as well in a Western meal as a Chinese one.

Jean Yueh
Summit, New Jersey

Serves 4 to 6

1½ pounds potatoes
4 tablespoons cooking oil
2 dried hot red pepper, broken in pieces
    and seeded, or 1 teaspoon crushed
    hot red pepper
4 cloves garlic, peeled and crushed
4 large scallions, including the green part,
    finely chopped
1 teaspoon salt

Peel the potatoes and cut into shreds the thickness of very fine matchsticks — the square-holed julienne disk on a food processor can be used. Rinse thoroughly with cold water, then drain and pat dry with paper towels.

Heat the oil in a wok over medium heat and fry the pepper until deep brown. Add the garlic and cook for about half a minute. Remove the garlic and pepper from the wok and discard, leaving the seasoned oil over heat.

Add the scallions to the hot oil and stir-fry for about half a minute. Add the potato shreds and salt, and stir-fry until the potatoes are slightly softened but still slightly crisp in texture, and serve at once.

Pilaf Mold

This pilaf can be cooked in individual molds, rather than one large one, if preferred.

Lynne B. Smith
Hanover, New Hampshire

Serves 6 to 8
Preheat the broiler; then preheat the oven to
   325 degrees

1 green pepper
7 tablespoons butter
1¼ cups minced onion
1½ cups long-grain rice
½ cup currants
3 cups hot chicken broth
1 tablespoon oil
½ cup sliced almonds
2 tablespoons grated Parmesan cheese
2 tablespoons minced parsley

Broil the green pepper on all sides until browned and blistered. Cool slightly, then peel off the charred skin and remove the stem, membrane and seeds, cutting the pepper into ½-inch squares.

Heat 3 tablespoons of the butter in a medium-sized heavy pan and gently sauté ¼ cup of the onion over low to medium heat for about 5 minutes, stirring often, not letting them brown. Stir in the rice and cook, stirring, for about 5 minutes. Add the currants and pour in the chicken broth. Bring to a boil, stirring to separate all the grains of rice. Reduce the heat to low, cover and simmer 15 to 18 minutes.

In a small pan heat the oil and 2 tablespoons butter, and sauté the remaining 1 cup of onion until golden. Add the almonds and cook until lightly colored.

When the rice is done, fluff with a fork and add the 3 tablespoons of softened butter, the Parmesan and the green pepper squares. Add the onion mixture and the parsley, and add more salt and pepper if needed.

Spoon the mixture into a buttered 6-cup mold, packing it tightly with the back of the spoon. Cover the mold with aluminum foil. At this stage the dish may be refrigerated overnight, or the cooking process can be completed.

Place the foil-covered mold in a bain-marie or a pan partly filled with warm water. Put in the preheated oven and cook for 20 to 30 minutes. Unmold onto a platter and serve.

Golden Beans
(Fagiolini Dorati)

These beans can be blanched and tied into bundles in advance and then finished just before serving. They make an attractive and unusual vegetable, appearing in individual portions. One pound of fresh beans will make nine to twelve small bundles.

Carlo Middione
San Francisco, California

Serves 4

12-15 long fresh chives, or scallion tops
1 pound fresh green beans
1 large egg, beaten
Salt
Pepper
Plenty of olive oil for frying
Flour for dredging

Blanch the chives, or scallion tops, for 30 seconds in about 2 cups of boiling water; drain.

Trim the beans, leaving them whole, and rinse under cold running water.

Bring about 6 quarts of water to a boil in a large pot. Drop the beans in, and let the water return to a boil. Cook over moderate heat about 3 minutes, possibly 4, but no longer. They should still be very crunchy. Drain and cool the beans.

When cool, assemble them into small bundles of 5 to 7 beans each and tie each bundle around the middle with a chive or scallion top. At this stage, they may be refrigerated to be fried later, or fried at once.

Pour the beaten egg into a dipping dish. Add salt and pepper and stir in. Heat the olive oil in a frying pan. Dip the bundles of beans in the egg, turning them in it, then roll them in flour. When the oil is very hot, fry the bundles until they are a golden color, taking care to keep the oil very hot, but not hot enough to overcook.

Transfer the bundles to paper towels to drain briefly, then serve at once.

Accordion Potatoes

These potatoes, after baking, will wait amiably in a low oven for a time, if you are not quite ready to serve. Garnish with parsley and cherry tomatoes and serve with steak or a roast.

Rubye Erickson
Edina, Minnesota

Serves 6 to 8
Preheat oven to 400 degrees

8 medium-size potatoes
8 tablespoons melted butter
2 teaspoons, or more, salt
Pepper
6 tablespoons grated Parmesan cheese
3 tablespoons breadcrumbs

Peel the potatoes and carefully slice each one very thinly without cutting down all the way through, to make them fan-shaped.

Put half the melted butter in an ovenproof serving dish and add the potatoes, fan side up. Sprinkle with salt and pepper and the remaining melted butter, being sure to get the seasonings and butter down between the slices.

Bake in the preheated oven about half an hour, basting frequently. Remove from the oven and sprinkle the combined cheese and breadcrumbs over each potato, again getting between the slices. Bake another 30 minutes, or a little longer if the potatoes are very large.

Deep-Fried Sage
(Salvia Fritta)

Here is a recipe for people who grow their own sage. The pungent leaves are encased in a batter lightened by folded-in egg whites; these cause the batter to puff up in the deep-frying. Fresh sage leaves can even be preserved in salt, which keeps them from drying out, and can then be used for this recipe, just like the fresh leaves are, after being rinsed in cold water and well dried with paper towels.

Giuliano Bugialli
New York, New York

Serves 8

BATTER:
1½ cups unbleached all-purpose flour
½ teaspoon salt
3 tablespoons olive oil
2 eggs, separated
Pinch of sugar
¼ cup pure alcohol, or vodka

About 50 fresh sage leaves
2 pounds solid vegetable shortening
Salt
Lemon wedges for garnish

Make the batter: Sift the flour into a large bowl. Make a well in the flour, then add, one at a time, the ½ teaspoon salt, the olive oil, egg yolks, sugar, alcohol, or vodka, and 1 cup cold water, mixing each in thoroughly before adding the next. When all the ingredients are incorporated, stir with a wooden spoon until the batter is smooth. Let stand in a cool place for about 2 hours. Set aside the egg whites to incorporate later.

Meanwhile, wash the sage leaves and pat them dry with a paper towel. Heat the vegetable shortening in a deep-fat fryer until very hot. Just before the fat is ready for frying, whip the egg whites, preferably in a copper bowl, until they are stiff. Fold them into the batter very gently with a rotating motion.

Dip each leaf of the sage in the batter and then quickly into the fat to cook for about 1 minute, until light and golden brown all over and very puffy. Remove and drain on paper towels while cooking the rest, draining each as it is cooked. When all are cooked, sprinkle with salt and serve hot, garnished with lemon wedges.

Salads

"Crisp" and "fresh" are the appropriate adjectives for the indispensables of a good salad — though the right combination of ingredients can also make an undetectible hiding place for leftovers. Dieters love salads and so do pennypinchers, and people in a hurry can throw together a salad lunch in no time. The variety of fresh produce available in markets everywhere has led to a general expectation in these times of a truly interesting salad on every occasion.

The recipes in this section promote these expectations and offer some interesting combinations. There is a salad of oranges and onions, one of potatoes and cauliflower. Palm hearts go with tomato, and roasted red peppers with zucchini. You'll find a spinach salad tossed in cognac dressing, fresh vegetables marinated Szechuan-style, and even a bringing together of carrots, peanuts and brandied grapes.

There will always be original ways to make a good salad, as long as there are original and creative cooks at work, and green shoots appearing in the spring.

Hearts of Palm Salad

Mary Blake Bryant
Austin, Texas

Serves 8

4 large tomatoes, cored and peeled
1 can hearts of palm

DRESSING:
1⅓ cups salad oil
½ cup wine vinegar
¼ teaspoon minced garlic
2½ teaspoons fresh basil
½ teaspoon dry mustard
1 teaspoon salt
½ teaspoon ground pepper

Bibb lettuce
¼ cup finely chopped onions
¼ cup finely chopped fresh parsley

Cut the tomatoes in half horizontally, and arrange in a shallow dish with the palm hearts, placing them together fairly tightly.

Make the vinaigrette dressing: Combine all the dressing ingredients in a jar and shake well. Pour the vinaigrette over the tomatoes and palm hearts and place in the refrigerator to marinate. Leave for about 3 hours, basting occasionally. At serving time, arrange the lettuce leaves on a platter, and put the tomato halves on the lettuce. Put the palm hearts on top of the tomato halves, sprinkle with chopped onion and parsley and spoon the vinaigrette over all.

Celery, Olive and Pickle Salad
(Insalata di Sedano, Olive et Cetrolini)

This is a salad which a creative Italian cook used to make during the winter months when she was unable to buy lettuce or tomatoes. The recipe is contributed by her daughter, who sometimes serves it to her own children as a treat.

Virginia Stefani
Pittsburgh, Pennsylvania

Serves 8

5 or 6 stalks celery, cut in ¼-inch slices
1 small can black olives, pitted,
   rinsed and drained
1 medium-sized jar sweet pickles,
   with their liquid
2 tablespoons olive oil
Salt
Pepper
1 can flat anchovies, drained

Put the celery in a bowl. Cut the olives in 4 slices each and the pickles in ¼-inch slices. Add to the bowl and pour about a third of the pickle liquid over them. Add the olive oil and toss the mixture. Add salt and pepper to taste, and arrange the anchovies over the top.

Potato and Cauliflower Salad
(Insalata di Patate e Cavalfiore)

Lenore Bleadon
Kentfield, California

Serves 6

2 large potatoes, with the peel left on
1 large cauliflower
1 sweet red pepper, peeled and cut in strips,
  or ½ cup sliced pimiento
Small handful fresh celery leaves,
  loosely chopped
10 small sprigs parsley, finely chopped
2 cloves garlic, minced
3 tablespoons anchovy paste
4 tablespoons red wine vinegar
½ cup olive oil
Salt
Pepper

Put the potatoes in a saucepan and cover with water. Cook, uncovered, for about 20 minutes or until tender. Drain and peel immediately. Let them stand until lukewarm.

In a saucepan filled with boiling salted water, cook the cauliflower for about 20 minutes, until cooked but not soft. Drain in a colander and let rest until lukewarm. Remove the florets from the central stem and arrange them in the center of a serving platter in a shape as much as possible like the original cauliflower head. Cut the potatoes into thin slices and arrange them in an overlapping circle around the cauliflower. Decorate the outer part of the platter with a ring of the red pepper strips or pimiento slices, and sprinkle the chopped celery leaves over all.

Mix and blend thoroughly the parsley, garlic, anchovy paste, vinegar, olive oil and salt and pepper, and pour over the cauliflower and potatoes. Let stand for 1 to 2 hours, and serve at room temperature.

Chicken and Pineapple Salad

Jane Armstrong
Melrose Park, Illinois

Serves 4
Preheat oven to 325 degrees

2 boneless chicken breasts
1 cup chicken broth

DRESSING:
½ cup mayonnaise
6 tablespoons plain yogurt
1½ teaspoons lime juice
¼ teaspoon curry powder

1 medium-size apple
8-ounce can crushed pineapple, well drained,
  juice reserved
1 tablespoon chopped onion
1 cup chopped celery
¼ cup salted peanuts

Place the chicken breasts and the broth in a casserole and bake, covered, for 45 minutes in the preheated oven.

Meanwhile, combine all the dressing ingredients, mix well and refrigerate.

Peel and core the apple and chop it. Put it in a small bowl with the juice from the pineapple.

Remove the chicken from the casserole and cool, then refrigerate. Set the broth aside for another use. When the chicken is cold, cut it into bite-sized pieces. Drain the apple and put in a bowl with the chicken, pineapple, onion, celery and peanuts. Toss with the dressing.

123

Szechuan Marinated Vegetables

This Chinese salad, a colorful mosaic of vegetables, keeps well under refrigeration for at least two weeks. The garlic and ginger may be removed after three or four days, since both tend to become stronger in flavor with time. Two other tips: the broccoli may darken with marinating, but its taste and texture will be unaffected. Other vegetables that may also be included are red and green peppers and cabbage cut in 1-inch squares; these will not need blanching. The number of hot peppers used will determine how spicy-hot the entire salad will be.

Susan Slack
Mission Viejo, California

Serves 10 to 12

1 medium-size head cauliflower in florets
1 bunch carrots, slant-cut in thick slices
1 bunch fresh broccoli, in florets
4-8 small hot red peppers
4 or 5 large cloves garlic, peeled and
    cut in half
1-inch piece ginger root, peeled and thinly sliced
1 cup sugar
1 cup white vinegar

Drop the cauliflower into boiling water. Stir once and pour into a colander. Rinse briefly under cold running water to stop it cooking.

Repeat this same blanching process with, separately, the carrots and the broccoli. Cool all three vegetables.

Cut the stems off the hot peppers and cut them lengthwise. Layer the three blanched vegetables in a large glass container with a tightly fitting lid, distributing the hot pepper slices, garlic pieces and ginger slices evenly among them.

Mix the sugar and vinegar with 2 cups of water and pour over the vegetables. Secure the lid, and store in the refrigerator at least 12 hours before opening.

To serve, remove from the container with a slotted spoon and arrange on a serving platter.

Stuffed Avocado Salad

This procedure requires a food processor. Both the cheese filling for the avocados and the Russian dressing can be made ahead of time and refrigerated overnight if desired.

Cookery & Company
Edie Acsell
Englewood, Colorado

Serves 10

FILLING:
12 ounces Edam or cheddar cheese,
  cut in pieces and chilled
½ cup mayonnaise
1 teaspoon dry mustard
2 teaspoons Worcestershire sauce
Dash of Tabasco sauce
2 tablespoons dry sherry
6 ounces cream cheese, softened

DRESSING:
1 cup mayonnaise
½ cup chili sauce
1 tablespoon Worcestershire sauce
Salt
Pepper

5 avocados, firm and ripe
10 large lettuce leaves
10 rusks

Make the filling for the avocados. Using a knife blade of the food processor, finely grate the cheese using on/off switch. Add the remaining filling ingredients and process until the mixture is smooth and pureed.

Make the Russian dressing. Again using the knife blade, blend together all the dressing ingredients.

At serving time, peel the avocados, cut them in half lengthwise and remove the seed. Fill the cavity with the cheese mixture. Put the avocado halves back together, cut into slices crosswise. Put a lettuce leaf on each serving plate, put a rusk on the lettuce and put avocado slices on the rusk. Spoon the Russian dressing over them and serve.

Roasted Red Pepper and Zucchini Salad

Marlene Sorosky's Cooking Center
Marlene Sorosky
Tarzana, California

Serves 8

DRESSING:
1 cup vegetable oil
¼ cup fresh lemon juice
¼ cup white wine vinegar
2 cloves garlic, crushed
2 teaspoons seasoned salt
1 teaspoon sugar
½ teaspoon dry mustard
½ teaspoon salt
¼ teaspoon crumbled dried red chili peppers

4 zucchini squash, sliced
½ cup sliced scallions, including green part
3 red peppers
½ pound spinach, well washed and drained

Put all the dressing ingredients together in a jar and shake well. Pour over the zucchini and scallions in a bowl, and marinate overnight.

A few hours before serving, preheat the broiler to the highest heat and broil the peppers about 4 inches from the heat, turning occasionally, until the skin is charred and almost black all over. Wrap the peppers in a tea towel and leave them to steam for about 5 minutes.

Transfer the peppers to a colander under cold running water. When cool enough to handle, remove the skins, which should slip off easily. Pat them dry and slice them into strips, discarding the seeds and pith. Add them to the bowl with zucchini and scallions and let marinate until ready to serve.

Tear the spinach leaves into bite-sized pieces. Toss the marinated vegetables well, and serve on a bed of the torn spinach leaves.

Spinach Salad with Cognac Dresssing

Lesand's
Louise Fiszer
Menlo Park, California

Serves 6

¼ pound Jerusalem artichokes, peeled
  and cut in ⅛-inch slices
1 tablespoon lemon juice
1 pound fresh spinach, well washed and
  drained, and stems removed
¼ pound mushroom caps, cleaned and cut
  in ¼-inch slices

DRESSING:
¾ cup walnut oil
5 tablespoons cognac
3 tablespoons cider vinegar
3 cloves garlic, crushed
½ teaspoon salt

Put the Jerusalem artichoke slices into a bowl with the lemon juice and 1 cup of water for a few minutes.

Tear the spinach leaves into pieces and put in a salad bowl. Pat the Jerusalem artichoke slices dry with paper towels, and add to the bowl. Add the mushroom slices.

Make the cognac dressing: Put all the dressing ingredients into a blender or food processor and blend at high speed for about 30 seconds.

Pour the dressing over the salad ingredients in the bowl, toss well and serve immediately.

Orange-Onion Salad

A tangy citrus salad is a good choice to go with rich meat and highly flavored main dishes. This one is also fine for picnics.

Zona Spray Cooking School
Zona Spray
Hudson, Ohio

Serves 6

1 Bermuda onion, thinly sliced
½ cup dry sherry, or Madeira

DRESSING:
¼ cup freshly squeezed lemon juice
¼ cup walnut oil or a bland vegetable oil
1 tablespoon honey
¼ teaspoon salt
Freshly ground white pepper

4 navel oranges
Parsley for garnish

Separate the onion rings and soak them in ice water for 5 minutes. Pat them dry and put in a bowl. Pour the sherry over them and let them marinate 2 hours or longer. Discard all but 2 tablespoons of the sherry marinade. Put this in a bowl and add all the dressing ingredients. Whisk to mix well.

Peel the oranges and cut in thin round slices, discarding the bits of core.

In a shallow dish, place alternate layers of orange slices and onion rings. Pour the dressing over them and refrigerate for half an hour longer. Serve garnished with parsley.

Carrot and Brandied Grape Salad

Preparing this unusual salad, which features grapes soaked in brandy, calls for a food processor.

Dorothy D. Sims
Tampa, Florida

Serves 6

1 cup seedless grapes
¼ cup brandy
1½ pounds carrots
6 ounces shelled peanuts
½ cup mayonnaise
½ cup cottage cheese
2 tablespoons lemon juice
3 tablespoons honey
1 pound spinach, well washed and drained, torn into bite-sized pieces
2 tablespoons slivered almonds

Place the grapes and the brandy in a jar with a tight-fitting lid, and refrigerate for a week.

Cut the carrots into 2-inch lengths. Insert the food processor's shredding disk, and pack the tube horizontally with the carrots. Using heavy pressure, shred them, then remove from the processor bowl.

Insert the knife blade and process the peanuts until a ball forms. Insert the funnel and, with the motor running, add the mayonnaise, cottage cheese, lemon juice and honey. Remove the knife blade and insert the plastic blade. With the motor on, add the carrots and process until well mixed. Add the brandied grapes and, using the on/off method, mix the grapes in.

Put the torn spinach into a salad bowl. Spoon in the salad mixture and garnish with slivered almonds.

Layered Vegetable Salad

This is an easy do-ahead salad.

Doris Koplin
Atlanta, Georgia

Serves 6

1 cucumber, peeled and diced
½ cup vinegar
1 pound fresh peas, shelled

DRESSING:
½ cup mayonnaise
½ cup sour cream
1 hard-boiled egg, finely chopped
2 tablespoons Parmesan cheese
2 tablespoons seasoned salt

4 stalks celery, diced
2-3 scallions, thinly sliced
¼ cup white or golden raisins
3 small carrots, peeled and diced
¼ teaspoon paprika, (optional)

Put the diced cucumber in a bowl and cover with vinegar. Leave for about an hour, then drain well. Cook the shelled peas in boiling water for 5 or 6 minutes. Drain.

Combine all the dressing ingredients and mix well.

Place half the peas in the bottom of a glass serving bowl. Then add, in layers, half each of the cucumbers, celery, scallions, raisins and carrots. Add a layer of half the dressing. Repeat the layering and end with a layer of the dressing on top. Sprinkle paprika over the dressing if desired. Refrigerate for at least 2 hours to chill thoroughly before serving.

Breads

The centrality of bread in the lives of most people on this earth is reflected in the bulk of this section of the book, in the variety of kinds of breads and ways of making and baking them that are included here, and in the detailed observations that follow in this introduction.

The range here includes breads of the many regions of America and of places far, far away, and the methods described are as various.

Of all the many techniques discussed here, all "work." However, each technique "works" in its own way and delivers its own result. One-rise yeast breads are characterized by an uneven texture, while multiple-rise breads produce a texture that is smooth and uniform throughout. Here are some further general observations that may be useful to you.

Gluten: Gluten is the protein in wheat, and in white wheat flours it constitutes almost the entire protein content. The correct flour-liquid ratio may vary as much as from 2 cups flour/1 cup liquid in the case of high-gluten flour to 3 full cups of flour/1 cup liquid for a low-gluten one. The gluten content of white wheat flours can be determined from the amount of protein indicated in the nutrition information on the package; a low-gluten flour will have about 9 grams of protein per cup of flour. Higher gluten content gives a nice elastic dough, which is desirable in yeast breads, while lower gluten content is desirable for cakes, pie crust, biscuits and muffins. For the latter, don't work the dough or batter much after the liquid has been added, to avoid results that are tough, but for yeast breads the kneading is essential for stretching (technically: "developing") the dough into elasticity.

Exact amounts: Yeast bread recipes presented here are purposely not precise as to exact amounts of flour and liquid. In addition to gluten content, which is the most important factor affecting the flour-liquid ratio, it also varies due to other differences in flours. Some consideration also must be given to local conditions, such as humidity and temperature, which will affect the behavior of dough where you live. You must learn to recognize when the dough is "right" and adjust recipes to fit your flour and local climatic conditions.

Additional rising: Be careful about additional rising — yeast bread that falls in the oven often has over-risen during the final rise; this additional rising in a hot oven can push the gluten beyond its elasticity and cause the collapse of the loaf.

Yeast tests: Yeast will keep its life in a freezing compartment and at any temperature lower than 140 degrees Fahrenheit; somewhere in the range between 140 and 150 degrees, the yeast will be killed. There are many ways to test ("proof") yeast for signs of life; here are two of them:

a) Dissolve yeast in warm water (100 to 120 degrees) with a pinch of sugar (which is food for the yeast) and watch for the formation of grey foam: if the foam appears/fails to appear, the yeast is live/dead.

b) Form a sponge of yeast, flour and a small amount of liquid, shape it into a ball and place in a bowl of warm water; if it rises, it is vital. (For exact method, see the French Walnut Bread recipe.)

Glazes: The darkness of a glaze is determined by its fat content. For a very dark and dull glaze, use egg yolk or butter, for their high fat content. For a light glaze with shine, use something with low fat content, such as egg white. For an intermediate color with shine, use a combination of egg yolk and white.

Rye Bread with Caraway

The Jewish rye bread flavor and look is produced by using white rye flour, which can be obtained from Jewish bakeries. Brushing with water gives rye bread a crisp crust. This bread freezes well, but then needs to be thoroughly reheated through. It is good spread with a strong garlic butter – eight to twelve cloves of garlic to a pound of butter is the proportion. An ice pick is handy for this recipe, preferably a stainless steel one which cannot rust.

Bailee Kronowitz
Savannah, Georgia

Makes 1 very large loaf
   or 2 medium-sized loaves
Preheat oven to 450 degrees
Flour a baking sheet

2 packages active dry yeast
1 tablespoon sugar
1½ tablespoons salt
2 cups whole rye flour, preferably white
10 cups all-purpose flour
2 to 3 tablespoons caraway seeds

Combine the yeast, sugar and salt in 1 quart warm water (110 degrees). Add the rye flour and mix. Add the all-purpose flour 1 cup at a time, mixing well. Add the caraway seeds. As soon as a movable mass has been formed, put the dough on a floured surface and knead it into a firm, non-sticking dough. Shape into a smooth ball and lay on the floured baking sheet. Let rise about 1½ hours.

Brush the risen bread all over with warm water and pierce with an ice pick in three places. Bake in the preheated oven for about 20 minutes. Remove from the oven and brush again with water all over the loaf. Turn down the heat to 425 degrees, put the bread back in the oven and bake another 20 minutes. Remove from the oven and if it has a slightly hollow sound when tapped, give it a final brushing with water, top and bottom, and put on a rack to cool.

Heidelberg Rye Bread

The Cook's Roost
Joanne B. Copeland
Fayetteville, North Carolina

Makes 2 loaves
Preheat oven to 375 degrees
Grease a baking sheet

3 cups whole wheat flour
2 packages active dry yeast
¼ cup carob powder
1 tablespoon caraway seeds
⅓ cup molasses
2 tablespoons butter
1 tablespoon sugar
1 scant tablespoon salt
3-3⅓ cups rye flour
1 tablespoon butter, melted

Mix the whole wheat flour, yeast, carob powder and caraway seeds in a large bowl. Heat 2 cups of water and add the molasses, butter, sugar and salt. Cook only until the butter is melted. Cool the mixture until just warm, then add to the large bowl. Beat slowly 1 minute, then faster for 3 minutes.

Stir in enough rye flour to make a good dough. Knead 5 minutes. Place in an oiled bowl, cover and let rise for 20 to 30 minutes. Punch down. Make two round loaves, slash the tops and brush them with melted butter. Let rise until doubled. Bake in the preheated oven about 30 minutes.

Challah Bread

This bread can be frozen, but should not be kept frozen for longer than a month. It is best served warm. To reheat, put it in a brown paper bag, sprinkle the bag with water and put in a moderate oven for ten or fifteen minutes.

Carmen Jones
Spring, Texas

Makes 2 large or 3 small loaves
Preheat oven to 375 degrees
Grease a baking sheet lightly

½ cup sugar
3 packages active dry yeast
9-11 cups high-gluten flour
1 cup egg yolks (10 to 12 yolks)
1½ tablespoons salt
½ cup oil
1 egg, beaten

Pour 2 cups warm water (110 degrees) into a large mixing bowl. Add the sugar and sprinkle the dry yeast over the water. Let stand for about 5 minutes until yeast is proofed. Add enough flour to make a thin dough, using a dough hook or beating by hand. Add the egg yolks, salt and oil. Mix thoroughly. Add enough of the remaining flour to make a medium-stiff dough and knead vigorously by hand for about 20 minutes, or if using a bread machine, for 10 minutes. Let rise in a covered bowl.

When risen, separate into two or three portions for the loaves. Separate each portion into five equal parts, and roll each into a short "rope." Braid the ropes, first moving the fifth rope over to a position between the first and second ropes, then moving the first one over two spaces to the right, then the second one, one space to the right, then repeating the sequence. Pinch the ends together securely and tuck under lightly. Place on the baking sheet side by side, covered, and let rise until doubled.

Mix the egg with 1 tablespoon water, and brush the loaves lightly with the mixture. Bake in the preheated oven until golden brown. Remove from the oven and cool thoroughly on a rack.

Easy Challah Bread

Lee R. Ehudin
Lutherville, Maryland

Makes 2 loaves
Preheat oven to 375 degrees
Grease 2 large baking sheets

4½ to 5½ cups flour
3 tablespoons sugar
1½ teaspoons salt
1 package active dry yeast
⅓ cup butter, softened
4 eggs, at room temperature
Poppy seeds

In a large electric-mixer bowl, mix thoroughly 1¼ cups of the flour with the sugar, salt, yeast and softened butter. Gradually add 1 cup of lukewarm (110 degrees) water and beat 2 minutes at medium speed, scraping the bowl occasionally. Add 3 eggs and 1 egg white, reserving the single yolk for glaze, and mix in ½ cup of the flour. Beat at high speed for 2 minutes, again scraping the bowl. Stir in enough additional flour to make a soft dough.

Turn out onto a lightly floured board and knead for 8 to 10 minutes, until smooth and elastic. Place in a greased bowl, turning to grease all surfaces. Cover and let rise in a warm place free from drafts, until doubled in bulk, 1 hour or more.

Punch the dough down and turn out onto a lightly floured board. Divide the dough in half, and form half the dough into a roll about a foot long. Divide it into six strands and braid, as follows: Labeling the six strands 1 to 6 from left to right, bring the outer two up and diagonally cross them, placing 6 over 1. Then cross 1 over both 4 and 5. Cross 2 over 3, 1, 4 and 5. Cross 6 over 3 and 1. Cross 5 over 3, 1, 6 and 4. Then repeat.

Place the loaf on one of the greased baking sheets. Repeat with the other half of the dough and place the second loaf on the second baking sheet.

Beat together the reserved egg yolk and 1 teaspoon of cold water. Brush the loaves with the mixture. Sprinkle with poppy seeds. Let rise again, uncovered, in a warm place until doubled in bulk, 1 hour or more. Bake in the preheated oven for 30 minutes. Remove and cool the loaves on a wire rack.

Dilly Cheese Round

This is a food processor recipe.

Jane Armstrong
Melrose Park, Illinois

Makes 1 loaf
Preheat oven to 350 degrees
Butter a round 9-inch cake pan

6 ounces cheddar cheese
1 ounce Parmesan cheese
¼ cup fresh parsley
1 package active dry yeast
¼ cup milk
1 tablespoon sugar
2 tablespoons butter or margarine
1 tablespoon minced onion flakes
1 teaspoon salt
2½-3 cups unbleached all-purpose flour
1 teaspoon dill weed
1 egg, beaten

With the processor's shredding disk, shred the cheddar cheese and transfer to a mixing bowl. With the knife blade, process the Parmesan for 10 seconds with on/off's, and transfer to the bowl. Put the parsley in with the knife blade and process for 5 seconds, until finely chopped. Add to the cheeses in the mixing bowl. Put the yeast, milk, sugar, onion flakes, salt and ¾ cup lukewarm water in the processor, and process for 5 seconds.

Add 1½ cups flour and the dill weed, and process until smooth. Add 1 cup flour to the cheese mixture and stir, then gradually add to the processor bowl, processing while adding, to form a stiff dough. Add the remaining flour if needed.

Remove from the processor bowl and knead 30 to 35 times. Cover and let rise in a warm place 1 hour. Punch down the dough and form into a ball. Place in the cake pan. Mix the egg with 1 tablespoon water and brush the dough with the mixture. Let rise until doubled in size, about 45 minutes. Bake in the preheated oven 20 to 25 minutes.

French Leek Bread

This is a food processor recipe. This bread will freeze satisfactorily.

Cookery & Company
Edie Acsell and Pat Miller
Englewood, Colorado

Makes 1 loaf
Preheat oven to 375 degrees
Grease a baking sheet or a 9-by-5-by-3-inch pan

1 packet leek soup mix
1½ tablespoons brown sugar
⅛ teaspoon salt
1 package active dry yeast
3 cups flour
1 tablespoon butter or oil
1 egg white, lightly beaten

With the processor's knife blade in place, put the leek soup mix, sugar, salt and yeast in the work bowl with 2¾ cups of flour. Process with on/off's to combine the dry ingredients. With machine off, add the butter or oil, turn it on and immediately add 1 cup of warm water. Process until the dough is smooth and pulls away from the sides of the bowl, keeping ¼ cup flour at hand to add if the motor begins to slow.

Continue to process for about 50 seconds longer, occasionally pulling the ball of dough apart and distributing it around the blade to knead, until it is no longer sticky and feels smooth and satiny. Place in an oiled bowl, turning once to oil the dough. Cover and put in a warm place to rise for about an hour, until doubled in bulk.

Punch down and roll to a rectangle about 12 inches by 15 inches. Roll out from the short side to form a smooth roll, pinching the seam and the ends well. Place seam side down on the baking sheet or in the loaf pan. Cover and let rise about 50 minutes, until almost double.

Mix the beaten egg white with 1 tablespoon of water and brush the loaf with the mixture. Make four or five diagonal slashes with a sharp knife across the top of the loaf about ¼ inch deep. Bake in the preheated oven 35 to 40 minutes, or until well browned. Cool on a wire rack.

Orange Breakfast Bread

...which is also very nice for afternoon tea.

The Tasting Spoon
Edith Gregg
Tucson, Arizona

Makes 1 loaf
Preheat oven to 375 degrees
Grease a loaf pan

1 cup orange juice
¼ cup sugar
¼ cup butter
1¼ teaspoons salt
1 package active dry yeast
1 egg, beaten
3¼ cups pre-sifted flour

In a saucepan combine the orange juice, the sugar, butter and salt and bring slowly to a boil. Remove from the heat to a cool place. When lukewarm, add the yeast and mix well. Add the beaten egg and the flour to make a dough. Knead for 10 minutes on a lightly floured board. Place in a lightly oiled bowl, turn once and cover with a damp cloth. Let rise until doubled in bulk. Return to the lightly floured board and knead 1 minute. Put in the loaf pan, cover and let rise 15 to 20 minutes.

Bake in the preheated oven 50 minutes to 1 hour. Remove and place on a rack to cool.

Herb Bread
(Pain Boule aux Herbes)

This is a good luncheon bread and makes an attractive addition to a buffet table.

Dorothy W. Crebo
Kokomo, Indiana

Makes 1 loaf
Preheat oven to 375 degrees
Grease, thoroughly, a round 8-inch cake tin with high sides

1 teaspoon chopped fresh oregano,
    or ¼ teaspoon dried oregano
1 teaspoon fresh thyme leaves, or
    ¼ teaspoon dried thyme
1 tablespoon chopped parsley
1 large clove garlic, minced
½ teaspoon freshly ground pepper
1 teaspoon salt
¼ cup olive oil
1 package active dry yeast
½ teaspoon sugar
¼ cup freshly grated Sardo or
    Parmesan cheese
¼ cup freshly grated Gruyère cheese
½ cup wheat germ
3½ to 4 cups unbleached all-purpose flour
2 eggs, beaten
1 egg white

Combine the oregano, thyme, parsley, garlic, pepper, salt and olive oil in a small bowl.

In a large mixing bowl, dissolve the yeast in 1 cup warm water, and add the sugar. In a third bowl, stir the two cheeses and the wheat germ into ½ cup of the flour.

Add the beaten eggs to the yeast mixture in the large mixing bowl, then add the herb mixture, then the cheese mixture, stirring well. Add the flour, ½ cup at a time, stirring to blend in. After adding nearly all the flour, turn onto a floured surface and knead the dough about 5 minutes, until smooth and well blended. Put into a greased bowl, turn once, and let rise about 1 hour, until doubled.

Punch down the dough, turn onto a lightly floured surface and let rest 5 to 10 minutes. Shape into as large a rectangle as possible. Trim the edges and roll lengthwise into a long tube. Coil it into the center of the cake tin. Cover with a cloth and let rise about 50 minutes, again doubling.

Mix the egg white with 1 teaspoon water, and brush the top of the dough carefully with it. Bake in the preheated oven 30 to 40 minutes, until the loaf is golden brown and pulls away from the tin. Run a knife around the edge to remove the bread from the tin, and put on a rack to cool. Serve at room temperature.

Oatmeal Spice Hearth Loaf

This bread, which is a "good keeper" with a dark brown crust and interesting texture, is particularly good if spread with butter while still warm from the oven.

Barbara H. Brown
Roswell, Georgia

Makes 1 large loaf
Preheat oven to 375 degrees
Grease a baking sheet

1 cup oatmeal (not the instant type)
2 tablespoons dark brown sugar
1 tablespoon molasses
2 tablespoons butter
½ cup raisins
1 cup all-purpose flour
1 cup stone-ground whole wheat flour
1 tablespoon active dry yeast
½ teaspoon ground cinnamon
¼ teaspoon allspice
1 tablespoon grated orange peel
1 teaspoon salt
1 egg, at room temperature
Melted butter for brushing

Put the oatmeal, sugar, molasses, butter and raisins in a bowl. Bring ⅞ cup water to a boil and pour the boiling water into the bowl; mix in well. With the knife blade in place in the processor, put both the flours, the yeast, cinnamon, allspice, orange peel and salt in the bowl. Process for 5 seconds. Add the egg and process with three or four on/off's. Add the lukewarm oatmeal mixture and process on/off three times, then run steadily for 35 to 40 seconds. Scrape down the sides of the bowl if necessary. The dough should be moist, and should form a shaggy ball on the blade. Transfer the dough to a floured board; do not be concerned if some of it is still in the bottom of the bowl — scrape out the bowl with a spatula if necessary. Knead for a minute or two, sprinkling with flour if sticky. The dough should be soft and easy to work. Form it into a ball. Place the dough in a warm buttered bowl, turning to grease all the surface. Cover with plastic wrap and put in a warm, draft-free place (about 80 degrees) for about an hour to double in bulk.

Punch down the dough, bringing the outside edges to the center. Turn out onto the floured board and knead several times. Smooth into a ball and place on the greased baking sheet, cover lightly with wax paper and put back in the warm place for about 45 minutes to double again.

Bake in the center of the preheated oven for 45 to 55 minutes. If the loaf seems to be getting too brown, place a sheet of foil lightly over it.

Remove from the oven and tap the bottom of the loaf. If it sounds hollow, it is done. Place on a cooling rack and brush the crust with melted butter.

Country Cinnamon Loaf

This is a good breakfast bread which toasts well. It is also a fine accompaniment for chicken salad, or fruit salad. The whole wheat berries used in making it can be found in health food shops; they are to be ground in an electric blender, not a food processor. Alternatively, they may be omitted and the stone-ground whole wheat flour quantity increased by half, in their place. A banneton (basket for bread rising) is useful in making this, as are oven tiles.

Shirley Waterloo
Hinsdale, Illinois

Makes 1 loaf
Preheat oven to 425 degrees
Grease a baking sheet and sprinkle with corn meal

¼ cup whole wheat berries
½ cup stone-ground whole wheat flour
¼ cup rolled oats (not instant or
   quick-cooking type)
1 package active dry yeast
2 tablespoons honey
½ cup buttermilk
1¾-2 cups all-purpose flour
2¼-2½ tablespoons safflower oil
1 teaspoon cinnamon
1½ teaspoons salt

Grind the whole wheat berries in an electric blender at high speed for a minute or two, until the hulls are thoroughly ground. Put in a bowl with the stone-ground whole wheat flour and the rolled oats.

In another bowl, dissolve the yeast in ¾ cup warm water. Add the honey, buttermilk and enough of the flour-oats mixture to make into a thick consistency that can be stirred without splashing. Use some of the all-purpose flour if necessary. Beat vigorously with a wooden spoon 100 times.

Let this sponge rest for at least 15 minutes, until bubbles form on the surface; or it may even stand for 2 or 3 hours at room temperature, or longer in the refrigerator. Add 2 tablespoons of the oil, the cinnamon, salt and enough of the remaining flour to make a stiff dough. Turn out on a lightly floured board and knead in all the remaining flour until smooth and springy, about 10 minutes. The dough should be moist.

Grease a bowl and a piece of waxed paper well with the remaining oil, and place the dough in the bowl, turning it to coat the entire surface with the oil. Cover with the oiled wax paper, then with plastic wrap. Let rise until doubled, about 2 hours.

Punch down. Knead a minute or two, adding a little additional flour if the dough is sticky. Let rest a few minutes. Work the dough into a ball, smoothing out the top and pinching together on the bottom.

Place on the prepared baking sheet to rise again, or in a well-floured banneton (if using a banneton, place the smooth side of the ball at the bottom of the basket, and after about an hour of rising, invert onto the baking sheet). Cover loosely with a towel and let rise until doubled and springy. Flour the loaf lightly.

Bake in the preheated oven for 10 minutes. Remove from the baking sheet very carefully and place on oven tiles. Continue to bake for 10 to 15 minutes longer, until the loaf is deeply colored and sounds hollow when rapped on the bottom. If tiles are not available, increase the final baking to 20 to 25 minutes and do not transfer it from the baking sheet until the final 3 minutes, when it should be baking on the oven rack without the baking sheet.

Butter Braid Bread

This is a food processor recipe. Take great care when adding the flour, as too much flour can ruin an otherwise well made loaf. The procedure given here is for two braided loaves. Alternatively the dough can be braided into one large loaf, or into a wreath, which will need a pizza pan to bake in. The double brushing with egg wash makes the crust an even golden brown.

Roxanna Young
Atlanta, Georgia

Makes 2 medium-sized loaves
Preheat oven to 350 degrees
Grease a baking sheet

1 package active dry yeast
½ cup milk
4 tablespoons butter
3 tablespoons sugar
1 teaspoon salt
2 eggs
3½ to 4 cups unbleached all-purpose flour
2 tablespoons melted butter
Poppy or sesame seeds
1 egg, beaten

Dissolve the yeast in ¼ cup warm water (110 degrees). Heat the milk until hot to the touch. Remove from the heat and add the butter, the sugar and the salt. Stir until the butter melts and sugar and salt dissolve. Cool. Add the 2 eggs. Beat to combine, then stir in the yeast mixture.

Place 2 cups flour in the processor with knife blade. Add the mixture from the pan and process until all the ingredients are thoroughly combined and the batter is smooth. Add 1 cup flour, processing until a ball forms. Continue processing for 30 seconds. Remove the lid and touch the mixture. If still sticky, add 1 tablespoon flour, process 30 seconds and check again. If necessary, add more flour, 1 tablespoon at a time, but cautiously, only until the dough is smooth and satiny looking, neither sticky nor dry and floury.

Place the ball of dough in a buttered ceramic bowl, cover with a towel, and let rise about 1 hour, until doubled.

Punch down, divide the dough in half, then divide each half into three equal parts. Roll each part into a rounded strip about a foot long. Braid three strips together as you would a pigtail. Press the ends together and tuck under, as you place it on the greased baking sheet. Repeat with the other strips to make the second loaf.

Brush the tops with melted butter and sprinkle with poppy or sesame seeds. Let rise in a warm place until double in bulk.

Mix the beaten egg with 1 tablespoon water, and brush the tops with half the mixture. Bake in the preheated oven for 20 minutes. Remove and brush again, with the other half of the egg mixture. Return to the oven and bake 10 to 15 minutes, or until golden brown.

French Walnut Bread
(Fougasse)

This bread should be placed to rise where the temperature does not exceed eighty degrees, or a sour, yeasty taste will result. At the table the bread is to be broken in pieces rather than sliced, and served with softened unsalted butter.

Cordon Rose Cooking School
Rose Levy Beranbaum
New York, New York

Serves 8
Preheat oven to 425 degrees
Oil a large baking sheet or an 18-by-12-inch jelly
    roll pan or a 14-by-16-inch pizza pan

3¼ to 3¾ cups unbleached all-purpose flour
1 package active dry yeast or
    ½ ounce cake yeast
¾ cup and 6-8 tablespoons skimmed milk
⅔ cup coarsely chopped walnuts
½ cup walnut oil
1½ teaspoons salt

Mix 1 cup of flour with the yeast and add 6 to 8 tablespoons skimmed milk, just enough to form a fairly soft ball of dough. Cut a cross into the top of the ball and drop it into a bowl of lukewarm water (110 degrees), and set aside. Within 15 to 35 minutes, the ball of dough should rise to the top of the water. If it does not, it indicates that the yeast was not active, and the procedure should be begun again with fresh yeast.

Meanwhile mix 2¼ cups of flour and the nuts in a large bowl. Make a sizable well in the center and add 2 tablespoons of the walnut oil, ¾ cup of the skimmed milk, and the salt. With a dough hook or wooden spoon, mix to form a fairly stiff dough.

When the dough starter has risen to the top of the water in the bowl, lift it from the water, shake it dry and add to the dough. Knead together for about 10 minutes, adding about ¼ to ½ cup of flour as needed to keep the dough from sticking. Knead until the dough is no longer sticky, and will retain the imprint of a finger.

Coat a large mixing bowl with 2 tablespoons of the walnut oil. Roll the dough in the bowl to coat all sides, and leave to rise about 1 hour, until doubled in bulk.

Punch down the dough and add 2 tablespoons of walnut oil. Knead lightly, and allow to rise a second time, until doubled again, about 40 minutes. Punch down again and allow to rise and double a third time, for about 30 minutes.

Punch down and roll out on the prepared pan. Allow to rise again, for about 15 minutes, but not to become more than ¾ inch high. Brush with the remaining 2 tablespoons walnut oil, and with a sharp knife cut 2-inch diagonal slashes about 2 inches apart all around the bread. With your fingers, push the slashes open. Bake in the preheated oven about 20 minutes, until crisp and brown.

Finnish Coffee Bread
(Nisu)

This bread is made with a food processor.

Shirley O. Corriher
Atlanta, Georgia

Makes 1 braided loaf
Preheat oven to 375 degrees

2 tablespoons sugar
1 package active dry yeast
½ cup warm milk (120 degrees)
2 to 3 cups flour (bread or unbleached)
½ cup sugar
1 teaspoon salt
1 tablespoon ground cardamom (seeds freshly
    crushed with a hammer)
6 tablespoons butter
2 eggs, at room temperature
2 tablespoons instant coffee stirred into
    3 tablespoons water
4 tablespoons sugar

Dissolve the sugar and yeast in the warm milk in a bowl. Place the steel blade in the processor bowl and combine 2 cups flour with the sugar, salt, cardamom and butter.

Process together for a few seconds to cut in the butter. Add the eggs and the milk-yeast mixture. Process with five or six on/off's. If the dough seems wet, add a little flour, just enough for the dough to form a ball. Process for a few seconds to let the ball of dough rotate 10 to 15 times. Place the dough in an oiled bowl, and turn it to coat it well with oil. Let rise in a warm place until doubled,

about 45 minutes. Punch down the dough and divide it into three portions. Shape each one into a long strand, and braid the three strands. Let it rise again in a warm place for 30 to 45 minutes. Bake in the preheated oven for 35 to 40 minutes, until the loaf sounds hollow when tapped on the bottom. While the loaf is warm from the oven, brush with the instant coffee mixture until the loaf becomes quite dark. While damp with coffee glaze, sprinkle with sugar.

Barese Scallion Bread

Marie Agresti
Franklin Square, New York

Makes 12 pieces 3 inches square
Preheat oven to 325 degrees
Prepare a 13-by-10-by-3-inch baking pan by
    pouring in ¼ cup of the olive oil

1 package active dry yeast
1 teaspoon sugar
1 teaspoon salt
1½ cups olive oil
3 to 3½ cups unbleached all-purpose flour
8 bunches scallions, washed, trimmed and
    cut in thirds
½ pound oil-cured black olives, pitted and
    cut in small pieces
4 cans flat anchovy fillets in olive oil
Freshly ground black pepper

Dissolve the yeast in warm water (about 110 degrees) in a large mixing bowl. Stir in the sugar, salt, 3 tablespoons of the oil and 2 cups of the flour. Beat until smooth. Stir in enough of the remaining flour to make the dough easy to handle. Turn onto a lightly floured surface. Knead until smooth, about 5 minutes. Place in a greased bowl and turn the dough to grease the entire surface. Cover and let rise in a warm place 45 minutes, or until an indentation remains when the dough is pressed with the finger.

Meanwhile sauté the scallions in ½ cup of the olive oil over medium heat until soft and limp.

Punch down the dough and roll into two large rectangles the size of the baking pan. Lay one rectangle on the floured surface. Arrange half the scallions and half the olives on the dough, and lay half the anchovies evenly on top of them. Grind pepper and dribble ¼ cup of the olive oil over the entire mixture.

Roll the second piece of dough on a rolling pin and gently lay it over the scallion mixture. Punch the two pieces together all around the edges. Place the remaining filling ingredients on top of the second piece of dough, in the same fashion, but omitting the oil.

Folding lengthwise, carefully lift the dough with two hands and fold over a quarter turn at one end. Do the same with the other end. Then turn the dough over again a quarter turn on both sides. You will then have reached the center, with all the filling covered by the dough. Fold over once more on one side. At this point there should be only one open fold showing. Beginning at one end, carefully start rolling the filled dough in one direction until you get to the end of the roll. Lift carefully and place, open-fold-side down, in the center of the oiled pan. Press down, spreading the mass of filled dough until it covers the whole pan. Pour the remaining oil over the entire top of the dough.

Bake in the preheated oven 30 minutes. Cover lightly with foil and bake another 30 minutes. Serve either warm or at room temperature.

Almond Cheese Ring

This is a food processor recipe. No substitute should even be considered in place of butter in this. The recipe can be doubled easily, and if another shape is preferred to a ring, it can be formed otherwise according to preference.

Susan Slack
Mission Viejo, California

Makes 1 ring to be cut in 10 to 12 portions
Preheat oven to 350 degrees
Grease a baking sheet

DOUGH:
½ cup sour cream
¼ cup sugar
½ teaspoon salt
4 tablespoons butter
1 egg
1 package active dry yeast
2 cups flour

FILLING:
8 ounces cream cheese
6 tablespoons sugar
Pinch of salt
1 teaspoon almond extract

ICING:
2 tablespoons butter
1¼ cups confectioners' sugar
½ teaspoon almond extract
1 to 2 tablespoons milk

8 maraschino cherries, well drained
32 to 48 toasted almond halves

Make the dough: Put the knife blade in the processor. Heat the sour cream in a pan over low heat. Add the sugar, salt and butter, and stir until the butter melts. Cool until lukewarm, then transfer to the processor bowl. Add the egg, processing in short on/off bursts. Dissolve the yeast in ¼ cup warm water (110 degrees) and add to the mixture. Process with one quick on/off. Add half the flour and process with one on/off. Add the other half of the flour, processing with on/off's then run the machine non-stop for about 10 seconds.

Remove the dough to a greased bowl, cover and refrigerate overnight.

Make the filling: Process all the filling ingredients until smooth. Roll out the dough into a rectangle about 12 inches by 16 inches. Spread the filling mixture on the rectangle and roll it up jelly-roll fashion, rolling the long side. Pinch the seam to seal, then form into a ring and join the ends smoothly to seal.

With scissors make cuts in the dough about 2 inches apart, cutting down about two thirds of the way through to the bottom. Gently swivel each cut section to the side slightly. Cover and let rise for about an hour. Bake on the greased baking sheet in the preheated oven for about 25 minutes.

Meanwhile make the icing: Melt the butter until light brown. Add the confectioners' sugar, almond extract and 1 tablespoon milk. Mix, and add more milk if needed to make the icing spreadable. Spread the mixture on the ring and decorate with flower shapes made of cherries for centers and almond halves as "petals."

Whole Wheat Bagels

Serve these split and toasted with cream cheese mixed with horseradish, or with unsalted butter and marmalade.

The Common Market School of Cooking
Donna Welsch
Cincinnati, Ohio

Makes 12 large or 24 small bagels
Preheat oven to 375 degrees
Grease two baking sheets

2 packages active dry yeast
2¾-3 cups high-gluten bread flour
3 tablespoons sugar or honey
1 tablespoon salt
1¼ cups stone-ground whole wheat flour
1 additional tablespoon sugar
1 egg, lightly beaten
Caraway or poppy seeds (optional)

In a large electric-mixer bowl, combine the yeast and 1½ cups of the bread flour. In another bowl, combine the sugar or honey and salt with 1½ cups of warm water (110 degrees) and add to the flour mixture. Beat until smooth. Beat in the whole wheat flour and enough of the remaining bread flour to make a moderately stiff dough. Knead on a floured surface 8 to 10 minutes, until smooth and elastic. Place in a greased bowl, turning to grease all surfaces. Let rise, covered, in a warm place for about 45 minutes.

Punch down and divide into 12 portions, or if miniature bagels are preferred, 24 portions. Punch a hole in the center of each with a floured finger. Pull gently to enlarge the hole to about 1 inch in diameter, or half that for the miniatures.

Place in an ungreased baking pan, cover loosely and let rise 20 minutes. Slide under the broiler 5 inches from the heat and broil 1 minute. Using a spatula, gently turn the bagels over and broil the other side for 1 minute.

Meanwhile, put 1 tablespoon sugar and 1 gallon of water in a large kettle and bring to a boil. Reduce heat to simmer. Drop the bagels in, a few at a time, taking care not to crowd the pan. Cook about 7 minutes (or half that time for miniature bagels), turning once. Remove with a slotted spoon and let drain. The bagels will be slippery. Place on the greased baking sheets. Mix the beaten egg with 1 teaspoon water, and brush the bagels with the mixture. If desired, sprinkle with seeds. Bake in the preheated oven 30 to 35 minutes, or until crusty and golden brown (15 to 20 minutes for the small ones). Transfer to a wire rack to cool.

Lemon Tea Bread with Icing

A very old family recipe is here adapted for a food processor.

Mary Jane Zirolli
Clifton, New Jersey

Makes 1 loaf
Preheat oven to 350 degrees
Butter an 8½-by-4-inch loaf pan

½ cup walnuts
1½ cups all-purpose flour
½ teaspoon salt
1 teaspoon baking powder
5 tablespoons unsalted butter
1 cup sugar
2 large eggs
½ cup sour cream or buttermilk
Grated zest of 1 lemon

ICING:
Juice of 1 lemon
½ cup of sugar

Using the knife blade of the food processor, chop the walnuts coarsely. Remove from the processor bowl and set aside.

Sift the flour, salt and baking powder together onto waxed paper.

Soften the butter in the food processor. Add the sugar and process to cream the two together. Add the eggs, and process until well mixed. Scrape down the sides of the bowl. Add the sour cream or buttermilk and the lemon zest. Process with several on/off bursts.

Carefully pick up the waxed paper with the dry ingredients on it, and form a chute with it to pour them into the bowl. Process with several on/off's.

Add the nuts and process just long enough to combine. Pour into the loaf pan and smooth the top. Bake in the preheated oven 1 hour or until a tester comes out dry and clean.

Meanwhile mix the lemon juice and sugar together well, for the icing.

Remove the tea bread from the loaf pan and ice the top while still warm from the oven.

Rum-Glazed Nutmeg Bread

This is a food processor recipe. Serve the bread slightly warm for breakfast or lunch. It is particularly good with fresh fruit.

Barbara Brown
Roswell, Georgia

Makes 1 large ring-shaped loaf
Preheat oven to 350 degrees
Butter an 8-cup ring baking pan thoroughly

12 tablespoons butter
3 tablespoons dark rum
1 cup pecans
½ teaspoon vanilla
1½ cups sugar
3 eggs, separated
2 cups and 1 tablespoon sifted
   all-purpose flour
2 teaspoons freshly grated nutmeg
1 teaspoon baking powder
1 teaspoon soda
¼ teaspoon salt
1 cup buttermilk, at room temperature
½ cup raisins

Chop the nuts coarsely in the food processor.

Melt 4 tablespoons of the butter over low heat, and stir in the rum. Add half the chopped nuts to the butter-rum mixture and stir to mix well. Pour into the buttered pan, making sure the mixture is evenly distributed around the bottom of the pan.

Cut the remaining butter in pieces, and add with the vanilla to the processor bowl. Start processing, and add the sugar, pouring slowly through the feed tube. Process until creamy. Add the 3 egg yolks, and process for about 5 seconds. Scrape down the sides of the bowl.

Sift 2 cups flour, nutmeg, baking powder, soda and salt together into a bowl.

Add half the flour mixture to the contents of the processor bowl and process in two or three quick on/off bursts. Add the buttermilk and process two on/off's. Add the rest of the flour mixture and process two on/off's.

Mix half the nuts and all the raisins with the remaining tablespoon of flour, and sprinkle over the batter. Process on/off once. Beat the egg whites until stiff, but not dry, in another bowl. Spoon about a third of the egg whites into the processor bowl and process on/off twice. Pour the contents of the processor bowl into the remaining egg whites, and fold in gently.

Pour the mixture into the pan and bake on the middle shelf of the preheated oven 40 to 50 minutes, or until a cake probe comes out clean.

Remove the pan from the oven. Place a sheet of foil over the cooling rack and carefully turn the loaf onto the foil. If any of the rum-nut mixture remains in the pan, spoon it up and place on the loaf. Serve while still warm.

Wild West Corn Bread

Wild indeed, this batter-type bread is filled with cheese and chili peppers and then baked.

Helen Augustine
Golden, Colorado

Serves 8 to 10
Preheat oven to 350 degrees
Grease a 9-inch-square baking pan.

1½ cups creamed corn
1 cup yellow cornmeal
1 cup melted butter
¾ cup buttermilk
2 medium-size onions, finely chopped
2 eggs, beaten
½ teaspoon baking soda
1½ to 2 cups grated cheddar cheese
3 jalapeño peppers, either fresh or
    canned, diced

Combine the corn, cornmeal, butter, buttermilk, onion, eggs and baking soda in a large bowl. Mix together well. Turn half the batter into the baking pan. Cover evenly with half the cheese, then all the peppers, the other half of the cheese and finally the rest of the batter.

Bake 1 hour in the preheated oven. Let cool for 15 minutes before serving.

Poppy Seed Bread

This is a sweet bread, especially good with fruit salad for lunch, or with morning coffee.

Mary Blake Bryant
Austin, Texas

Makes 2 loaves
Preheat oven to 350 degrees
Line two loaf pans with wax paper

6 eggs
2 cups sugar
1½ cups cooking oil
2 cups all-purpose flour
2 teaspoons baking powder
½ teaspoon salt
½ box (1 ounce) poppy seeds
½ cup milk and cream (half-and-half)

Beat the eggs. Add the sugar and oil, and beat well. Combine the flour, baking powder, salt and poppy seeds, and add to the mixture alternately with the half-and-half, stirring well. Divide into the two loaf pans and bake in the preheated oven about 1 hour, until lightly browned.

Nut Puff Breakfast Sweet

Donna Adams
New York, New York and Cleveland, Ohio

Serves 6 to 12
Preheat oven to 350 degrees
Grease a baking sheet

8 tablespoons butter
2 cups flour
⅞ to 1⅛ cup cold milk
¼ to ½ cup chopped pecans, almonds or
    walnuts, or a mixture
½ cup sugar
3 large eggs
1 teaspoon vanilla extract
½ cup confectioners' sugar

Cut the butter into 1 cup of the flour until the mixture resembles cornmeal. Add 2 tablespoons of cold milk, and knead lightly. Put in the refrigerator to rest. After 15 minutes, remove and divide the dough in two. Roll out into two strips about 12 inches long and 3 inches wide. Sprinkle the strips with most of the nuts and all the sugar. Refrigerate again.

In a saucepan bring 2 cups of water and ½ cup of milk to a boil. Add the remaining flour, beating it in until a ball forms. Add the eggs, one at a time, beating each one in well. Stir in the vanilla. Spread half of this mixture over each of the strips, on top of the nuts and sugar. Put the strips on the baking sheet and bake in the preheated oven 1 hour. Let cool.

Make the frosting: Combine the confectioners' sugar with enough of the remaining cold milk to make a thin, but not too runny, mixture. Cover the strips with it, and sprinkle the rest of the chopped nuts over the top.

Blueberry Muffins

Several groups of cooking school students aged seven to twelve voted this recipe their all-time favorite.

Susan Manlin Katzman
Clayton, Missouri

Makes 24 muffins
Preheat oven to 350 degrees
Grease two 12-muffin pans

3 cups all-purpose flour
2 cups sugar
1 tablespoon baking powder
10 tablespoons butter
2 eggs
1 cup evaporated milk, undiluted
1 teaspoon vanilla extract
1¾ cups blueberries, well washed and
    with stems removed

Mix the flour, sugar and baking powder in a large mixing bowl. Cut in 8 tablespoons of the butter with a pastry blender or with two knives handled scissors-fashion. Reserve 1 cup of this mixture for the crumb topping.

Add the eggs, milk and vanilla to the remaining mixture in the bowl. Beat with an electric beater until smooth.

Gently fold the blueberries into the batter with a spatula, and immediately spoon the batter into the muffin cups, dividing it equally among them.

Melt the remaining butter in a small saucepan. Dribble the melted butter over the reserved crumb mixture and toss with a fork. Sprinkle the buttery crumb mixture on the tops of the batter in the muffin cups, again dividing equally.

Bake in the preheated oven 20 to 30 minutes, until the muffins are a light golden brown. Remove from the oven and let the muffins cool a little before removing them from the pans.

Honey-Glazed Bran Muffins

These fruited muffins are nutritious and freeze well. They should be served warm.

Shirley Rubinstein
Cinnaminson, New Jersey

Makes 12 muffins
Preheat oven to 400 degrees
Line a 12-muffin pan with paper baking cups

1 cup bran
1 cup buttermilk
1 cup all-purpose flour
1 teaspoon baking powder
½ teaspoon baking soda
1 teaspoon ground cinnamon
½ teaspoon salt
⅓ cup butter, at room temperature
½ cup brown sugar
1 large egg
¼ cup molasses
⅓ cup raisins
⅓ cup chopped dates

GLAZE:
¾ cup honey
⅓ cup corn syrup
1 tablespoon butter

Combine the bran and buttermilk in a medium-sized mixing bowl. In another bowl, mix together the flour, baking powder, baking soda, cinnamon and salt. Add this dry mixture all at once to the bran mixture. Stir only enough to mix.

Cream the butter, brown sugar, egg and molasses together and stir into the bran mixture. Stir in the raisins and dates, and spoon the mixture into the muffin cups, filling each one three-quarters full. Bake in the preheated oven 20 to 25 minutes.

Meanwhile combine the glaze ingredients in a small saucepan over medium heat and bring to a boil. Reduce heat and simmer for 5 minutes.

When the muffins are done, cool them slightly, removing the paper if you wish. Dip each one upside down in the glaze to coat the tops thoroughly. Serve as soon as the glaze is set.

Nanny's Light Southern Biscuits

The secret of light biscuits is actually three secrets: a very wet dough, a very hot oven and soft winter wheat flour, with a low gluten content. This is a food processor recipe. Three alternative methods of shaping the biscuits are given.

Shirley Corriher
Atlanta, Georgia

Makes 12 biscuits
Preheat oven to 500 degrees
Grease a baking sheet

1½ cups self-rising flour, sifted
1 teaspoon salt
¼ teaspoon soda
3 to 4 tablespoons vegetable shortening
¾ to ⅞ cup buttermilk

With the knife blade in the processor, add the flour, salt and soda by processing with quick on/off's. Add the shortening and process until the mixture becomes the texture of cornmeal. Add ¾ cup buttermilk and process again with a few on/off's, stopping as soon as the dough is mixed. It should be very wet (add more buttermilk if it is not). Do not overprocess or the biscuits will be tough.

To shape the biscuits, use the drop-biscuit, hand-shape or cut-biscuit method.

For drop biscuits, drop one tablespoon of wet dough at a time onto the greased baking sheet, leaving space between.

For hand-shaped biscuits, flour the fingers, pick up a biscuit-size ball of wet dough and roll it in flour. Slightly flatten it to shape and place on the greased baking sheet.

For cut biscuits, pour the dough onto a clean, well-floured tea towel of close-woven fabric. Fold one end of the floured tea towel over on top of the dough and press out gently until the dough is about ½ inch thick. Dip a cutter into flour and cut the dough from above straight down. Place the biscuits on the greased baking sheet as you cut them, and reflour the cutter before cutting each one.

Bake in the preheated oven for 8 to 10 minutes, or until brown.

Indian Bread
(Poori)

This is an ideal bread to serve with curry dishes.

Lillian Marshall's School for Cooks
Lillian Marshall
Louisville, Kentucky

Serves 6

Oil for deep-frying
1¼ cups all-purpose flour
1¼ cups whole wheat flour
6 tablespoons butter
½ teaspoon salt

  Preheat the oil in a deep fryer to 375 degrees. Combine the flours in a mixing bowl. Add the butter and rub it in with the fingers until the mixture resembles coarse cornmeal. Add the salt. Slowly add cold water, stirring with a fork, until a firm dough is formed. Turn out on a floured surface and knead briefly to smooth the dough. Cut into 6 equal pieces and roll out each piece into an uneven circle about ⅛ inch thick.
  Deep-fry until golden brown and drain on absorbent paper.

Outrageous French Toast

This is so simple! – but sometimes the simplest is the best. The special ingredient that makes this French toast wonderfully puffy is baking powder. The dish is prepared the night before. Serve with jam, syrup or powdered sugar, or offer all three choices.

Rona Cohen
Bethesda, Maryland

Makes 6 toasts

3 large eggs, beaten
½ cup milk
2 tablespoons sugar
⅛ teaspoon baking powder
Generous pinch of ground cinnamon
6 thick slices bread
2 to 3 tablespoons butter

  Combine the eggs, milk, sugar, baking powder and cinnamon in a bowl. Put the bread slices in a 9-by-13-inch baking dish and pour the mixture over them, turning so that each slice becomes coated on both sides. Cover the pan with wax paper and press the paper down slightly on the soaking bread to "seal" it. Refrigerate overnight.
  When ready to cook, heat the butter in a large skillet and fry the bread slices, making sure not to crowd them in the pan. Cook until golden brown on both sides and serve hot.

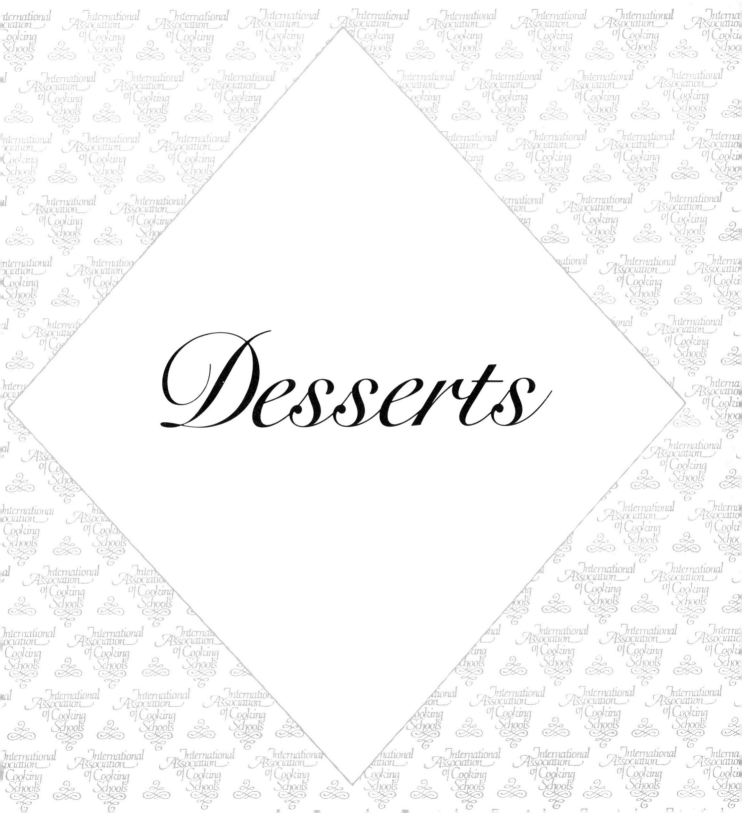

Desserts

The desserts offered in this section date in origin from 18th century colonial America to even earlier traditional dishes that graced European tables long before egalité was ever thought of. Dessert is as frivolous and unnecessary as the lady who is said to have said, "Let them eat cake." It is an extravagance, an extra sensation. People always need bread, but they never need dessert. The realization of deliberate excess is the wooing charm of this part of one's meal.

Of course, you must balance your menu. The dessert you are offering must be compatible with the meal you are serving. A rich main course calls for a light dessert. Vice versa, a light entree invites you to consider a grand finale. Whichever it is, make it wicked and memorable.

The desserts in this chapter are appropriate climaxes for any meal. Consider the abundance of approaches — crêpes, cookies, candies, mousses, fruits, tortes, tarts, munchies, snacks, pastas, bars, filo, cakes, soufflés, meringues, yeast doughs, parfaits, pôts de creme . . .

This is the moment for your meal's last impression — so make it last.

Lemon Soufflé Crêpes

These crêpes may be made ahead of time. The filling may also be prepared ahead, up to the addition of the egg whites, which should be held off until shortly before serving time.

Sharon Lane
Irvine, California

Serves 10 to 12
Preheat oven to 425 degrees

CRÊPE BATTER:
1 cup flour
1 tablespoon sugar
3 large eggs
2 cups milk
½ teaspoon salt
2 tablespoons butter, melted and cooled

FILLING:
4 tablespoons butter
½ cup sugar
Juice of 2 lemons
Grated peel of 2 lemons
4 egg yolks
5 egg whites
Confectioners' sugar for sprinkling

With an electric mixer, food processor or a whisk, blend all the batter ingredients, adding the melted butter last. Cover and set aside for at least 30 minutes.

Make the filling: Heat together the butter, ¼ cup of the sugar and the lemon juice and peel. Cook until the butter is melted and the sugar dissolved. Remove from the heat. Add the 4 egg yolks to the pan, one at a time, and return it to low heat, stirring until the mixture thickens to the consistency of heavy cream.

At the end of 30 minutes, make the crêpes, using a 6-inch or 7-inch crêpe pan.

Half an hour before serving, beat 5 egg whites with the remaining ¼ cup of sugar until stiff. Gently reheat the lemon mixture to lukewarm, and fold in the egg white mixture.

Spoon a small amount of the filling onto the center of each crêpe, and fold two sides over to cover the filling. Bake in the preheated oven 12 to 15 minutes, or until puffed. Sprinkle with confectioners' sugar and serve immediately.

Pumpkin Cheesecake

Lillian Marshall's School for Cooks, Inc.
Lillian Marshall
Louisville, Kentucky

Serves 16
Preheat oven to 400 degrees

CRUST:
6-ounce box zwieback, in fine crumbs
⅓ cup sugar
2¾-ounce jar candied ginger, finely minced
8 tablespoons butter, melted

FILLING:
4 packages (8 ounces each) cream cheese, at room temperature
1¾ cups sugar
¼ cup flour
Grated zest of 1 lemon
16-ounce can pumpkin
6 eggs, beaten
2 cups sour cream

⅓ cup honey

Make the crust: Mix together the zwiebach crumbs, sugar, ginger and melted butter. Reserve about one third of the mixture. Spread the rest of the mixture into a 9-inch springform pan, pressing it firmly onto the bottom and about a third of the way up the sides of the pan. Reserve the rest of the mixture.

Make the filling: Blend together the cream cheese, sugar, flour, lemon zest, pumpkin, eggs and ¼ cup of the sour cream. Pour the mixture into the crust, and bake in the preheated oven for 15 minutes. Reduce heat to 225 degrees and bake 1½ hours longer, or until set.

Remove from the oven, leaving it set at 225 degrees, and spread the remaining sour cream over the top of the cheesecake. Sprinkle the reserved crumb mixture over the sour cream, and return the cheesecake to the oven. Bake 10 minutes longer. Cool on a rack, still in the pan. Refrigerate overnight.

Remove from the pan and drizzle the honey over the top before serving.

Frozen Raspberry Mousse

This can be made with strawberries and a strawberry liqueur rather than raspberries, if preferred. It can also be made without the cream, for dieters. And instead of the tablespoon of kirsch, half a teaspoon of almond extract may be substituted.

Irene Rothschild
Elkins Park, Pennsylvania

Serves 10 to 12

10-ounce package frozen raspberries, thawed
¾ cup sugar
2 egg whites
1 tablespoon lemon juice
Pinch of salt
1 tablespoon kirsch
1-1½ cups whipping cream
Chopped pistachio nuts for decoration (optional)

Combine the raspberries, sugar, egg whites, lemon juice and salt in an electric mixer bowl. Beat for 15 minutes, until pale pink and stiff. Add the kirsch. Whip 1 cup of cream and fold in.

Spoon the mixture into a soufflé dish or individual ramekins, and freeze.

Whip the rest of the cream and decorate the mousse with whipped cream rosettes, and the pistachios, if desired.

Hazelnut Blitz Torte

This torte has three elements: cake, which is baked in two layers; meringue, which tops each layer; and cream filling, which is placed between the two meringue-topped layers. The torte may be made ahead, but should not be assembled until a few hours before serving. The praline paste for the cream filling is available in specialty food shops, or instant coffee may be substituted. Alternatively, praline powder may be used instead, but as it is less concentrated, the amount should be increased by half. A final tip: the torte should not be covered, or the meringue will sweat.

Carole Walter
Emerson, New Jersey

Serves 10 to 12
Preheat oven to 325 degrees
Generously butter and lightly flour two 9-inch cake
    pans with removable bottoms

CAKE:
1 cup sifted cake flour
1 teaspoon baking powder
⅛ teaspoon salt
8 tablespoons unsalted butter,
    at room temperature
½ cup sugar
4 egg yolks, well beaten
1 teaspoon vanilla extract
3 tablespoons milk

MERINGUE:
4 egg whites, at room temperature
½ cup sugar
⅓ cup confectioners' sugar
½ teaspoon vanilla extract

PRALINE CREAM FILLING:
3 egg yolks
¼ cup sugar
2 tablespoons cornstarch
1 tablespoon flour
1 cup milk
2 tablespoons praline paste
⅓ cup heavy cream, whipped
½ teaspoon vanilla extract

½ cup coarsely chopped hazelnuts
1 tablespoon sugar

Sift the flour, baking powder and salt together. Cream the butter and add the sugar gradually, creaming them together. Add the egg yolks and beat them in well. Add the vanilla extract and stir in. Gradually add the flour mixture, alternating with additions of the milk, stirring each addition in well.

Make the meringue: Beat the egg whites only until they stand in peaks. They should not become dry. Add all the sugar of both kinds except for 1 tablespoon of granulated sugar, adding it 1 tablespoon at a time, beating in well. Add the vanilla extract and beat all together until stiff and glossy.

Spread half the cake batter in each of the prepared pans, and spoon half the meringue over each, making certain that the entire surface is covered while the meringue clings to the sides of the pan. Sprinkle the top of the meringue with nuts and the remaining tablespoon of sugar. Bake in the preheated oven 30 to 35 minutes or until the surfaces are lightly browned. (The torte expands during baking, and will shrink and sink slightly in the center when cool.) Place on cake racks to cool, and remove from the pans after they have cooled completely.

Make the filling: Whisk the yolks and sugar together in a saucepan until light. Stir in the cornstarch and flour, and mix well. Combine the milk and praline paste, and whisk into the filling mixture gradually. Place the saucepan over low heat and cook, stirring constantly, as it thickens. Just as it is reaching the boiling point, remove from the heat and pour into a bowl. Cover with buttered wax paper and let cool, then refrigerate. When chilled, fold in the whipped cream and vanilla extract.

To assemble the finished torte, place a cake layer on a serving platter, meringue side up. Spread the meringue carefully with the cream filling, leaving half an inch uncovered around the edges. Place the second cake layer on top, meringue side up. Chill until ready to serve.

Fresh Banana Cake

Karen D. Benner
Houston, Texas

Serves 6 to 8
Preheat oven to 350 degrees
Butter and lightly flour an 8-inch square baking pan

8 tablespoons butter
1⅓ cups sugar
1 cup mashed ripe bananas
2 eggs
1 teaspoon vanilla extract
2 cups cake flour
1 teaspoon baking soda
½ teaspoon salt
½ cup buttermilk
Confectioners' sugar for sprinkling

Cream the butter, slowly adding the sugar. Beat until light. Add the bananas, eggs and vanilla, beating in well.

Mix the flour, baking soda and salt. Add to the first mixture and stir together. Slowly add the buttermilk, beating until it is well incorporated.

Spread into the prepared pan and bake in the preheated oven 45 minutes, or until a tester comes out clean. Cool for 5 minutes in the pan, then turn upside down onto a rack, and sprinkle with confectioners' sugar.

Linzer Torte

This version of an old European favorite keeps well; it tastes even better after a week or so. It makes a fine do-ahead party dessert, served with whipped cream.

Hermie Kranzdorf
Narberth, Pennsylvania

Serves 10 to 12
Preheat oven to 375 degrees
Butter and flour a 9- or 10-inch shallow pan with removable bottom

11 ounces butter
5 ounces sugar
3 hard-boiled egg yolks
11 ounces flour
1 ounce cocoa powder
3 ounces almonds, toasted and ground
Grated zest of 1 lemon
½ teaspoon cinnamon
½ teaspoon cardamom
1-2 tablespoons kirsch
⅔ jar red raspberry preserves
1 egg, lightly beaten

Work together the butter, sugar and hard-boiled egg yolks in a bowl until they are well blended. Mix in the flour, cocoa powder, ground almonds, lemon zest, cinnamon and cardamom. Add enough kirsch to form a smooth dough. Work the dough thoroughly, with a mixer or by hand.

Wrap the dough well in waxed paper and then in a plastic bag; refrigerate for several hours or overnight. Remove from the refrigerator about an hour before needed.

Roll out half the dough on a lightly floured board and place in the tart pan to cover the bottom and the sides.

Fill with the raspberry preserves to form a thin smooth layer.

Roll out the rest of the dough into a rectangle and cut it in half-inch strips. Form the strips into a lattice pattern on top of the tart. Brush the lattice crust with a little of the beaten egg, and place on a baking sheet. Bake in the preheated oven 35 to 40 minutes.

Remove from the oven and let cool in the pan to room temperature.

Remove the tart from the pan, wrap well and store in the refrigerator for a day or two to mellow before serving. Serve at room temperature.

Chocolate Truffles

Marion B. Sullivan
Columbia, South Carolina

Makes about 4 dozen small candies

PRALINE:
1 cup pecans, or almonds or hazelnuts, with
    skins removed, or a mixture
1 cup sugar

1¼ pounds semi-sweet chocolate
3 egg yolks
8 tablespoons unsalted butter,
    at room temperature
2 tablespoons dark rum
8 ounces roasted hazelnuts, with skins removed

Make the praline: Brown the nuts in a slow oven until well toasted. Put the sugar in a heavy saucepan with 4 tablespoons of water and cook until the mixture starts to color. Watch carefully and remove as soon as it reaches a caramel color. Stir in the nuts and pour at once onto an oiled baking sheet with sides or onto a marble slab. Let cool completely, until hard and dry. Then pulverize in a blender or food processor.

Melt 3 ounces of the chocolate; let cool slightly. Beat in the egg yolks. Stir in the butter and rum. Add the praline and stir. Chill.

Rolling a little of the chilled mixture around one hazelnut for each, make about 48 small balls. Chill thoroughly.

Gently melt the 12 ounces of chocolate. Dip the truffles in the chocolate and place on wax paper to harden. Refrigerate if necessary to firm the coating.

Colonial Hermit Cake

This dense fruity cake is especially good with cream cheese. It will keep for up to two weeks in the refrigerator. Preparation of this recipe starts two days before you wish to serve the cakes.

The Happy Cooking School, Inc.
Dolores Kostelni
Lexington, Virginia

Makes 20 to 24 slices
Preheat oven to 275 degrees
Grease and lightly flour a 10-inch tube pan

1½ pounds chopped dates
½ pound dried apricots, coarsely chopped
1 pound mixed nuts, coarsely chopped
Juice of 1 lemon
1 cup orange juice
5 cups sifted flour
2 cups unsalted butter
2½ cups dark brown sugar
8 eggs
2 teaspoons vanilla extract
4 teaspoons baking powder
½ teaspoon salt
2 teaspoons cinnamon
1 teaspoon freshly grated nutmeg

In a large bowl, combine the dates, apricots and nuts and pour the lemon and orange juice over them. Mix. Cover and let stand overnight.

Stir 1 cup of the flour into the bowl with the fruit and nuts, and set aside. In another bowl cream the butter and brown sugar together until light and fluffy. Add the eggs one at a time, beating in well. Add the vanilla.

Sift together the remaining flour, the baking powder, salt, cinnamon and nutmeg, and add a little at a time to the butter-sugar-egg mixture. Beat in well after each addition. Add the fruit and nut mixture and stir in thoroughly.

Spread the mixture evenly in the tube pan and bake in the preheated oven for 2½ to 3 hours, or until a tester, inserted in several places, comes out clean. Let stand for a day before serving.

Chocolate Torte

This flourless "cake" is pure pleasure for chocoholics. It will freeze well without the frosting. To halve the recipe, use eight-inch pans.

Libby Hillman's Cooking School
Libby Hillman
Great Neck, New York and
  Wittingham, Vermont

Serves 12 to 16
Preheat oven to lowest (100-140 degrees)
Line two round 9-inch pans with rounds of wax
  paper cut to fit and stuck to the bottom with
  dabs of butter

8 ounces unsweetened chocolate
1 cup unsalted butter, at room temperature
3-3⅛ cups confectioners' sugar
8 eggs, separated
1 cup chopped walnuts or pecans
1 cup heavy cream
Shaved chocolate for decoration

Set the chocolate in a bowl in the preheated oven to melt. Reset the oven to 350 degrees.

Beat the butter in the bowl of an electric mixer, gradually adding the confectioners' sugar. When light and fluffy, add the egg yolks, beating constantly. Stir in the chocolate. Beat the egg whites until stiff and fold them into the chocolate mixture. Remove a third of the mixture and set it aside as a filling. Stir the chopped nuts into the remaining batter. Spoon equal amounts of the nut batter into the prepared cake pans and smooth the tops. Bake 17 minutes.

Remove the pans from the oven and run a knife around the inside rim to loosen the cakes. Place a rack over one of the pans, and, using pot holders, quickly invert the cake onto the rack. Repeat with the other cake and a second rack. The cakes should come out of the pans easily. Remove the waxed paper and let the cakes cool.

Spoon the reserved filling onto the top of one of the cakes, and place the other one on top. Whip the cream with the remaining 2 tablespoons of confectioners' sugar (or omit the sugar if preferred). Frost the top and sides of the cake with the whipped cream and decorate with shaved chocolate curls.

Savarin

This rum-soaked cake may be served with a sweetened whipped cream into which have been folded fresh strawberries or raspberries. Alternatively, it can be decorated with whipped cream rosettes, each encircling one fresh berry; or in the holiday season, it can be decorated with candied cherries and angelica. The batter in this recipe may also be used to make babas au rhum, by filling small baba molds about two-thirds full, placing them on a baking sheet in a moderate oven for about twelve minutes, then dipping them into syrup and brushing with glaze, as here.

John Clancy's Kitchen Workshop
John Clancy
New York, New York

Serves 10 to 12
Preheat oven to 400 degrees
Grease a 6-cup Savarin mold thoroughly

½ cup milk, lukewarm
1 package dry yeast
3 tablespoons sugar
2 cups flour
4 eggs, lightly beaten
½ teaspoon salt
12 tablespoons unsalted butter, softened

SYRUP:
1 cup sugar
½ cup dark rum

GLAZE:
1 cup apricot preserves
2 tablespoons dark rum (optional)

Put the warm milk in a bowl. Add the yeast and ½ teaspoon of the sugar. Set aside to proof for 6 to 8 minutes.

Place the flour, beaten eggs, salt and the remaining sugar in a mixing bowl. Add the yeast mixture, and with a wooden spoon, or a mixer fitted with a flat paddle, beat together into a soft batter. Cover the bowl and let rise until doubled, about 45 minutes.

Stir the batter down and beat in the softened butter, 2 tablespoons at a time. Spoon into the prepared mold and let rise again. When almost doubled, put in the preheated oven and bake for 10 minutes. Reduce heat to 350 degrees and bake for about 30 minutes longer, until golden brown.

Turn out on a rack set in a jelly roll pan to cool slightly.

Make the syrup: Combine the sugar and 2 cups water in a saucepan. Stir over low heat until the sugar is dissolved. Wash down the sides of the pan, raise heat and boil for 5 minutes. Remove from the heat and add the rum.

Spoon the syrup over the cake.

Make the glaze: Heat the apricot preserves and force through a sieve. Add the rum, if desired.

Spoon the glaze over the cake, and let cool.

Pear Custard Tart

This is best served the day it is made. It should not be frozen.

Hermie Kranzdorf
Narberth, Pennsylvania

Serves 10 to 12
Preheat the oven to 375 degrees

CRUST:
1¼ cups flour
2 tablespoons sugar
Pinch of salt
12 tablespoons butter
1 egg
1½ teaspoons water

CUSTARD:
⅔ cups sugar
1 tablespoon cornstarch
1 egg, beaten
¾ cup sour cream
¾ cup heavy cream
Juice of ½ lemon
½ teaspoon vanilla extract

½ cup breadcrumbs or cake crumbs
5 to 6 pears, peeled, cored and cut in
    slices ½ inch thick

Make the crust: Blend the flour, sugar and salt together. Work the butter into the flour mixture until small crumbs form. Mix the egg with the water, and combine with the mixture, stirring together just until a dough is formed. Shape into a ball. Flatten it slightly, wrap and refrigerate for at least 30 minutes.

Roll the dough out and line a 9-inch tart tin 1¼ inches deep with a removable bottom. Chill for 10 minutes in the refrigerator.

Make the custard: Mix the ⅔ cup sugar and the cornstarch together in a bowl. Add the beaten egg and stir. Add the sour cream, heavy cream, lemon juice and vanilla extract and beat until smooth.

Sprinkle the breadcrumbs or cake crumbs into the chilled pastry shell. Put the pear slices on top of the crumbs, and pour the custard mixture over the pears. Bake in the preheated oven for 1¼ hours, or until the filling is set and the pears are tender. Serve either chilled or at room temperature.

Orange Amaretto Tart

The pastry shell can be made and baked with the apricot preserves a day in advance. However, the tart should be filled with the almond cream and orange glaze the day it is to be served. This is an excellent dessert to serve with a duck dinner.

Nancy Kirby
Lake Bluff, Illinois

Serves 8
Preheat oven to 375 degrees

CRUST:
1½ cups flour
Pinch of salt
1½ tablespoons sugar
8 tablespoons unsalted butter, chilled
1 egg yolk
3-4 tablespoons cold water

¼ cup apricot jam

ORANGE GLAZE:
1 cup orange juice
1 cup sugar

2 large thick-skinned oranges

ALMOND CREAM FILLING:
2 egg yolks
6 tablespoons sugar
4 tablespoons unsalted butter
½ cup ground blanched almonds

¼ cup Amaretto liqueur

Make the crust: In a bowl combine the flour, salt and sugar. Mix well. Cut the butter into small pieces and work it in with a pastry blender until the mixture forms particles the size of very small peas. Beat the egg yolk with 3 tablespoons of water. Make a well in the center of the flour-butter mixture and pour in the egg mixture. First mix with a fork, then press the dough into a ball with the hands. Add more water if necessary to get it to come together. Flatten the dough into a thick pancake shape. Wrap in wax paper and chill for at least half an hour in the refrigerator.

Roll out the pastry to a thickness of ⅛ inch, and line a 9-inch tart tin. Prick the bottom with a fork.

Heat the apricot jam just to warm, and if there are any large pieces of preserves in it, cut them up. Spread the preserves over the unbaked crust. Refrigerate for 15 minutes.

Bake in the preheated oven for 12 to 15 minutes, until the crust is lightly colored and draws away from the sides of the pan. Remove from the oven and let cool. Raise the oven temperature to 400 degrees.

For the glaze, slowly heat the orange juice and the sugar together in a saucepan, and when bubbling, let simmer for about 20 minutes. Wash the oranges well and wipe dry. Leaving the peel on, cut them into thin slices. Discard the bits of core in the centers. Add the orange slices to the syrup in the saucepan, return to a simmer and cook over very low heat another 10 to 15 minutes, until all are well glazed with syrup. Remove the orange slices with a slotted spoon and spread on a rack, reserving the syrup.

Make the filling: Beat the egg yolks until light. Gradually beat in 3 tablespoons of the sugar and mix until thick and pale yellow. Cream the butter and the remaining 3 tablespoons of sugar. Beat the yolk mixture into the creamed butter-sugar mixture. Stir in the ground almonds.

Fill the cooled tart shell with the filling and bake in the preheated 400-degree oven for 10 to 12 minutes, until the center of the filling is set and light golden brown. Let cool.

Boil the reserved orange syrup until it is the consistency of a glaze, bearing in mind that it will thicken as it cools. Remove from the heat and stir in the Amaretto.

Arrange the orange slices over the filling in the tart in overlapping circular rows. Spoon the warm syrup over the oranges. Let the tart cool completely before serving. (It tastes best when cool but not served directly from the refrigerator.)

Chestnut and Chocolate Pôts de Crème
(Pôts de Crème Turinois)

Donna Nordin
San Francisco, California

Serves 8
Preheat oven to 350 degrees

1 cup milk
1½ cups heavy cream
5 egg yolks
5 tablespoons sugar
2 tablespoons rum
4 ounces semi-sweet chocolate, melted
½ cup unsweetened chestnut puree
Whipped cream for decoration
  (optional)
Chocolate shavings (optional)

Stir together the milk, cream, egg yolks, and sugar. Add the rum. Blend the melted chocolate with the chestnut puree and beat into the egg mixture. Pour into pôts de crème dishes or small ramekins, and set them in a baking pan with about ½ inch of hot water in it. Place carefully in the preheated oven. Bake about 45 minutes. Let cool. Chill for about 2 hours before serving. Decorate with whipped cream and chocolate shavings, if desired.

Chocolate Amaretto Mousse Torte

Marlene Sorosky's Cooking Center
Marlene Sorosky
Tarzana, California

Serves 10 to 12

CRUST:
1½ cups Amaretti cookie crumbs
6 tablepoons butter, melted

1¼ pounds semi-sweet chocolate
4 egg yolks
2 eggs
¼ cup Amaretto liqueur
6 egg whites
½ cup confectioners' sugar
3½ cups heavy cream

Make the crust: Mix the crumbs and the melted butter, and press the mixture into the bottom of a 9-inch springform pan. Refrigerate.

In the top of a double boiler over hot but not boiling water, melt 1 pound of the chocolate. Remove from the heat and let cool for 10 minutes.

Add the 4 yolks one at a time to the mixture, stirring them in with a wooden spoon, then add the 2 whole eggs, one at a time. Stir in the Amaretto liqueur.

Beat the 6 egg whites in a mixing bowl until soft peaks form. Slowly beat in the confectioners' sugar, 1 tablespoon at a time, until the mixture stiffens. In another bowl, whip 2 cups of the cream until soft peaks form.

Fold alternately the whipped cream mixture and the egg white mixture into the chocolate mixture. Pour the mousse into the prepared crust and refrigerate.

Melt the remaining 4 ounces of chocolate and pour into the bottom of a 9-inch-square metal baking pan. Refrigerate.

When the chocolate has hardened but is still pliable, make curls of it, using a spatula. (If the chocolate breaks, it's too cold. Leave at room temperature until it will bend. If the chocolate sticks, it needs to be refrigerated longer.)

Shortly before serving, whip the remaining 1½ cups of cream until stiff. Remove the sides of the springform pan. Spread about half of it thinly on top of the torte. Using a pastry bag with a large star tip, pipe rosettes with the rest of the whipped cream around the edges.

Decorate the surface of the whipped cream with the chocolate curls.

Pecan Pie

This pie may be served with lightly sweetened whipped cream.

Lee Barnes Cooking School
Lee Barnes
New Orleans, Louisiana

Serves 6 to 8
Preheat oven to 375 degrees

5-6 tablespoons butter, softened
¾ cup firmly packed brown sugar
3 eggs
½ cup light corn syrup
1 cup chopped pecans
1 teaspoon vanilla extract
¼ teaspoon salt
1 prebaked 8-inch pie shell
Pecan halves for decoration

Cream together the butter and brown sugar. Beat in the eggs one at a time. Stir in the corn syrup, chopped pecans, vanilla extract and salt. Mix well. Fill the pie shell with the mixture and decorate with pecan halves. Bake in the preheated oven for 30 minutes.

Fruit Cake Cookies

These cookies are to be prepared a day ahead.

Cook & Co.
Larry W. Brown
Nashville, Tennessee

Makes about 10 dozen cookies
Preheat oven to 275 degrees

4 eggs
1 cup sugar
8 tablespoons unsalted butter
1 cup flour
2 teaspoons baking powder
Pinch of coarse salt
2 tablespoons bourbon
½ pound candied pineapple, chopped
½ pound candied cherries, chopped
1 pound pitted dates, chopped
1 pound pecans, chopped

Beat together the eggs, sugar and butter in a large mixing bowl. Sift together the flour, baking powder and salt, and add to the mixture. Stir in the remaining ingredients, cover and refrigerate overnight.

Drop by teaspoonfuls onto ungreased baking sheets and bake in the preheated oven about 25 minutes, no longer.

Sweet Sponge Pastries
(Zeppole Dolci)

This is one of the traditional dishes prepared by Italians for special feast days. To make the pastries spoonfuls of batter are dropped into hot oil to cook. A tip for helping the batter to slide easily off the spoon is to dip the spoon first into the hot oil, then the batter, repeating for each spoonful. Another good idea is to deep-fry one first by itself, then cool and taste it to be sure it is cooked through. This will help in determining the timing for the rest. These may be frozen without the sugar and cocoa coating — add this before serving. If further decoration of the pastries at the end is desired, colored sugars or nonpareils may be scattered on top.

Nell Benedict
Lathrup Village, Michigan

Serves 8 to 10

4 tablespoons unsalted butter
⅛ teaspoon salt
½ teaspoon grated orange peel
¼ teaspoon grated lemon peel
1 cup flour
¼ teaspoon nutmeg
4 large eggs
1 tablespoon sugar
1 to 1½ cups confectioners' sugar
1 to 1½ tablespoons unsweetened cocoa
Oil for frying

Put 1 cup of water in a medium-sized saucepan over high heat. Add the butter, salt and orange and lemon peels. Bring to a boil and remove from the heat. Add the flour, all at once, and the nutmeg.

Stir until well incorporated. Return to the heat and cook, stirring, until the mixture forms a ball. Remove from the heat and let cool slightly. Add 2 eggs and beat well. Add the other 2 eggs and beat again. Add the sugar and mix in thoroughly.

Mix 1 cup of the confectioners' sugar and 1 tablespoon of the cocoa by shaking it together in a paper bag. Reserve in the bag.

In a deep saucepan or fryer, pour oil to a depth of 3 to 4 inches and heat to 375 degrees (or until it is hot enough to brown a cube of bread in 1 minute). Drop the batter into the oil by teaspoonfuls and fry, three or four at a time, until deep golden brown on all sides. Remove with a slotted spoon and drain on paper towels, then shake them in the bag with the sugar and cocoa, adding more sugar and cocoa to the bag as needed, until they are all well coated.

Georgia Blackberry Jam Cake

Frances Neel
White, Georgia

Serves 6 to 8
Preheat oven to 375 degrees
Line a loaf pan or square baking pan with
    oiled paper

3 cups sifted flour
¾ teaspoon cinnamon
¾ teaspoon nutmeg
½ teaspoon salt
12 tablespoons butter,
    at room temperature
2 cups brown sugar
2 eggs, well beaten
1 teaspoon baking soda
1½ cups buttermilk
1 cup blackberry jam
1¼ cups chopped pecans
1 cup raisins
Confectioners' sugar for sprinkling (optional)

Sift together the flour, cinnamon, nutmeg and
salt. Cream together the butter and brown sugar
until the mixture is very light. Stir in the eggs.
Dissolve the baking soda in the buttermilk and
add, a little at a time, to the mixture, alternately
adding the flour mixture a little at a time. When
all the ingredients are mixed together, fold in the
blackberry jam, pecans and raisins.

Pour into the lined pan and bake in the
preheated oven for about 50 minutes, or until the
cake tests done. Cool on a rack and sprinkle with
confectioners' sugar before serving, if desired.

Chocolate Nut Pie, Microwave

Alice Copeland Phillips
Atlanta, Georgia

Serves 8

9 tablespoons butter
1¼ cups graham cracker crumbs
1⅛ cups sugar
½ pound cream cheese
⅓ cup heavy cream
6-ounce package semi-sweet chocolate bits
2 tablespoons flour
¼ teaspoon salt
¾ cup chopped pecans
1 teaspoon vanilla extract

In a pie plate, microwave ½ cup of the butter at
70% of full power for 1 minute. Reserve 2
tablespoons of the crumbs and blend the rest with
2 tablespoons of the sugar and the melted butter.
Press the mixture firmly into the pie plate to form a
crust. Microwave for 1 to 2 minutes on high power.
Let cool.

In a bowl mix the cream cheese, heavy cream,
chocolate bits and the remaining 1 tablespoon of
butter. Microwave on 70% power for 2 to 3
minutes, until melted. Take the bowl from the oven
and add the remaining ingredients. Mix well. Pour
the mixture into the pie shell. Microwave again on
70% power for 5 to 6 minutes, until set. Sprinkle
with the reserved 2 tablespoons of crumbs, and let
cool before serving.

Filbert Soufflé

The Eight Mice Cooking School
Lafayette, Indiana

Serves 4 to 6
Preheat oven to 400 degrees

3 tablespoons flour
¾ cup milk
⅓ cup plus 1 tablespoon sugar
4 eggs yolks
5 egg whites
2 tablespoons butter, at room temperature
2 teaspoons vanilla extract
¾ cup ground toasted filberts
Pinch of salt

In a saucepan whisk the flour with a little of the milk to blend. Beat in the rest of the milk and the ⅓ cup sugar and cook, stirring, until the mixture thickens and comes to a boil. (The sauce will be very thick.) Remove from the heat and continue whisking a little longer, to cool slightly.

Separate the eggs and set one yolk aside for another use. Add the remaining 4 yolks to the cooled mixture, stirring in one at a time. Then add the butter and the vanilla. Stir in the ground nuts. Beat the 5 egg whites with the pinch of salt, and fold carefully into the filbert mixture. Pour into a 4-cup soufflé dish. Place in the oven and immediately turn the heat down to 375 degrees. Bake about 30 minutes.

Pillow Cookies

Cynthia Berland
Chicago, Illinois

Makes 4 dozen cookies
Preheat oven to 375 degrees

½ pound unsalted butter, at room temperature
¾ cup sugar
1 egg
2 teaspoons vanilla extract
2¼ cups flour
½ teaspoon salt
1 large package assorted miniature chocolate bars

Cream the butter. Beat in the sugar. Add the egg and vanilla and continue beating until the mixture is thick and lemon-colored. Stir in the flour and salt and beat until well blended.

Divide the dough in half. Fit a cookie press with a saw-tooth plate and fill with dough. Press the dough onto ungreased baking sheets in the form of strips about 3 inches long, until half the dough is used.

Place one tiny chocolate bar on each strip. Press the other half of the dough out in strips onto the tops to cover the chocolate completely. Bake in the preheated oven for about 10 minutes, until golden brown. Cool slightly, then place on racks to cool.

Poached Pears in Chocolate Sour Cream Sauce

When pears are in season, this recipe can be prepared frequently, in which case the poaching liquid could be reused, rather than having to be discarded. Refrigerate it in a tightly closed jar between times. The chocolate sour cream sauce is also an ideal dipping sauce for strawberries or orange slices, as it hardens when it is cooled. It may also be served at room temperature, and a further variation, if desired, is to serve the pears hot.

Sara E. Sharpe
Miami, Florida

Serves 6

2 cups sugar
1 vanilla bean, split
1 stick cinnamon
6 firm nearly ripe pears, preferably Boscs

SAUCE:
6 ounces semi-sweet chocolate
⅓ cup orange blossom honey
⅓ cup Grand Marnier
1 cup sour cream

Put the sugar in a saucepan with 6 cups of water. Bring to a boil. Add the vanilla bean and cinnamon stick. Reduce the heat and let cook gently for a few minutes, to steep. Meanwhile, peel and core the pears, leaving them whole. Lower them into the simmering liquid and poach them until almost tender. There should be just a bit of resistance when one is pierced with the point of a sharp knife. Remove from the heat and let the pears cool in the poaching liquid. Then refrigerate, still in the liquid. When almost ready to serve, drain them thoroughly.

Meanwhile, make the sauce: In a small saucepan, heat the chocolate and the honey together. When melted, whisk in the Grand Marnier and the sour cream. Heat almost to the boiling point. Pour the sauce, very hot, into a shallow plate, and place the pears on top.

White Chocolate Mousse with Mint Sauce

White chocolate is a synthetic chocolate, so special care should be taken when melting it and mixing it with other ingredients.

Anne Otterson
La Jolla, California

Serves 6

2 tablespoons butter
8 ounces white chocolate, chopped
   into small bits
1½ teaspoons unflavored gelatin
3 egg yolks
1 cup heavy cream
1 tablespoon vanilla extract
4 egg whites
1 tablespoon sugar

SAUCE:
8 ounces German chocolate, chopped
   into small bits
1 cup heavy cream
1 tablespoon crème de menthe liqueur

Put about an inch of water in a large pan into which a small saucepan can be fitted, and bring to a boil.

In the small saucepan melt the butter and add the white chocolate. Cover the pan and set it into the larger pan containing the boiling water. Immediately turn off the heat.

Add the gelatin to 2 tablespoons of cold water and stir.

In a heavy stainless steel or enamel saucepan whisk 3 egg yolks until thick. Add the cream and stir over low heat just until the mixture thickens. Do not overheat or the eggs will curdle. Remove from the heat and add the gelatin mixture, stirring until dissolved. Add the chocolate mixture and whisk vigorously until smooth. Add the vanilla.

Whisk the egg whites to soft peaks. Add the sugar and continue whisking until the peaks are stiff and shiny. Fold a small portion of the egg whites into the chocolate mixture to lighten. Then fold in the rest. Pour into a soufflé dish or serving bowl and chill.

Make the sauce: Put the German chocolate bits in a heavy saucepan with the cream. Cook over low heat, stirring, until the chocolate melts and the sauce is smooth. Add the crème de menthe and stir.

Form the mousse into oval shapes like quenelles, three per serving. Pour a small amount of the sauce onto each dessert plate, and place the three "quenelles" of mousse on each one, in spoke-like fashion.

Ginger Soufflé
(Soufflé à l'Indienne)

This dish can be partially prepared three or four hours ahead of time. After adding the ginger, rub the surface of the soufflé mixture with butter to prevent a skin forming in the interim.

Carol's Cuisine
Carol Giudice
Staten Island, New York

Serves 8
Preheat oven to 425 degrees
Butter a 2-quart soufflé dish

6 egg yolks
¾ cup sugar
½ cup flour
2 cups milk, scalded
1 teaspoon ground ginger
2 tablespoons preserved stem ginger, chopped
8 egg whites
Confectioners' sugar for sprinkling

Beat together the egg yolks and half the sugar until thick and light. Stir in the flour, then whisk in the scalded milk. Mix well. Return the mixture to the saucepan. Cook over moderate heat until it comes to a boil. Simmer, whisking constantly, about 2 minutes, or until the mixture has thickened. Stir in the ground ginger and the chopped preserved ginger.

Beat the 8 egg whites until stiff. Add the remaining sugar and beat 20 seconds, until glossy. Reheat the ginger mixture until hot to the touch. Remove from heat and stir in about a quarter of the egg whites. Add the mixture to the remaining egg whites and fold them together as lightly as possible. Spoon the mixture into the prepared soufflé dish. Smooth the top and bake immediately in the preheated oven for 20 to 30 minutes, or until puffed and brown. Sprinkle with confectioners' sugar and serve at once.

Fruit Fritters

This recipe has proved popular with aspiring cooks as young as eight years of age.

The Silo
Tony and Gail Diminico
New Milford, Connecticut

Serves 6

BATTER:
2 eggs, separated
½ cup milk
2 tablespoons sherry
1 tablespoon oil
1 cup all-purpose flour
1 tablespoon sugar
Pinch of salt

Oil for frying
1 box strawberries
½ fresh pineapple, cubed
1 apple, peeled, cored and cubed
Confectioners' sugar for sprinkling

Make the batter: Combine the egg yolks, milk, sherry, oil, flour, sugar and salt. Mix well. Cover and refrigerate for about 3 hours. Remove from the refrigerator and leave at room temperature for 20 minutes. Beat the egg whites just until stiff. Fold the egg whites into the batter.

Meanwhile, heat the oil for deep-frying in a wok or deep saucepan. Dip the pieces of fruit into the batter and deep-fry until golden. Drain and sprinkle with confectioners' sugar.

Almond Crescent Cookies

This is a food processor recipe. These cookies will keep well in sealed jars.

Roxanna Young
Altanta, Georgia

Makes 3 dozen cookies
Preheat oven to 350 degrees
Grease 2 baking sheets lightly

1 cup blanched almonds
½ pound butter, cut into very small pieces
½ cup sugar
1 teaspoon vanilla extract
½ teaspoon salt
2 cups flour
Confectioners' sugar for dusting

Chop the almonds in the food processor with the steel blade. Remove the almonds from the bowl. Soften the butter in the food processor. Add the sugar and process until the mixture is light and creamy. Add the vanilla, salt and flour. Process until combined. Return the nuts to the bowl and process only until they are incorporated into the mixture. Transfer the mixture to a bowl, cover and refrigerate for half an hour.

Shape the dough, a tablespoonful at a time, into short cylinders about ½ inch thick. Bend them into crescent shapes and place on the baking sheets about an inch apart. Bake 15 to 20 minutes in the preheated oven. The cookies should be dry when they are cooked, but not browned. Cool slightly, then dust with confectioners' sugar.

Chocolate Imperiale

This cake is very rich indeed — small portions are advised. It may be made and glazed the day before serving, but should not be refrigerated.

Flo Braker
Palo Alto, California

Serves 12
Preheat oven to 375 degrees
Grease and flour an 8-inch springform pan and
    line the bottom with a circle of wax paper
    or parchment

4 ounces semi-sweet chocolate
8 tablespoons butter
⅔ cup sugar
Grated zest of 1 orange
1 tablespoon Grand Marnier
3 eggs
2 cups ground walnuts

GLAZE:
6 ounces semi-sweet chocolate
6 tablespoons butter
1 tablespoon light corn syrup

Put the 4 ounces of chocolate and 8 tablespoons of butter in a saucepan over low heat and stir as it melts. Add the sugar and the orange zest and mix in. Transfer to a mixing bowl and let cool about 5 minutes.

Add the Grand Marnier and then the eggs, mixing each in but not beating. Add the ground walnut "flour" and lightly mix all together. Pour into the prepared pan and place on the middle rack of the preheated oven. Bake for 25 minutes. Check to see if it is done. It should not bake dry because it will firm a bit as it cools, but it may still be too fudgelike. If so, bake for another 5 minutes.

Cool in the pan before removing the sides. Turn the cake upside down on a rack and remove the paper. Let it cool completely before glazing.

Meanwhile melt the 6 ounces of chocolate and 6 tablespoons of butter over hot, but not boiling, water. Stir in the corn syrup. Pour carefully over the cake, gently tilting the pan to help the glaze flow over the entire top and down the sides, and keeping a little of the glaze in the pan. Reheat the remaining glaze, pour into a paper cone and on top of the cake write the word: Imperiale.

Hamentashen

A traditional gift to carry when calling on friends or relatives in Germany is a covered plate of these fruit-filled pastries.

What's Cooking!
Phyllis Frucht
Rockville, Maryland

Makes 30 pastries
Preheat oven to 400 degrees
Grease 2 baking sheets

PASTRY:
2 cups all-purpose flour
¾ cup sugar
2 teaspoons baking powder
¼ teaspoon salt
½ cup vegetable shortening
2 tablespoons orange juice
1 egg, beaten

FILLING:
10 ounces prunes, soaked and chopped
⅔ cup raisins
1 apple, peeled, cored and grated
½ teaspoon lemon juice

1 egg, beaten
1 teaspoon sugar
Generous pinch of cinnamon

Make the pastry: Sift together the flour, sugar, baking powder and salt. Work in the shortening with the fingers. Add the orange juice and beaten egg; mix well. Chill overnight, or for at least 2 hours.

Roll the dough out to ⅛-inch thickness. Cut into 3-inch rounds.

In a bowl combine all the filling ingredients, and put a heaping teaspoonful of the mixture on each round. Bring up the edges on three sides and pinch together at the top.

Place the three-cornered packets of pastry and filling on the greased baking sheets. Brush the beaten egg over them and sprinkle sugar and cinnamon over. Bake in the preheated oven for 20 minutes. Cool on a rack.

Nubian Chocolate Torte

This cake can be made a day in advance, and refrigerated overnight; it should be served well chilled.

Barbara Pullo
Suffern, New York

Serves 8
Preheat oven to 350 degrees
Grease a 15-by-10-inch baking pan, and line with greased parchment paper or greased wax paper cut to fit

3 eggs, separated
5 tablespoons sugar
3 tablespoons unsweetened cocoa
1 teaspoon vanilla extract
½ teaspoon almond extract
½ teaspoon ground cinnamon
¼ teaspoon aniseed

FILLING:
2 cups heavy cream
¼ cup sugar
2½ tablespoons unsweetened cocoa
½ teaspoon vanilla extract
¾ cup walnut halves

Beat the egg yolks well. Add the sugar, a tablespoon at a time, beating each one in. Stir in the cocoa, vanilla and almond extracts, cinnamon and aniseed. Beat the egg whites until stiff, and fold gently into the cocoa mixture. Spoon into the prepared baking pan and bake in the preheated oven 20-25 minutes.

Meanwhile, make the filling: Combine all the filling ingredients except the walnuts in an electric-mixer bowl, and chill for 15 minutes. Then beat at high speed until well mixed.

Turn out the cake and remove the parchment. Let cool. Cut into three layers. Spread a third of the filling and a third of the nuts on each of the layers, then carefully stack the layers. Spread the remaining cream and nuts on the top layer. Chill until ready to serve.

Strawberry-Rhubarb Parfaits

These may be topped with rosettes made from additional heavy cream, whipped stiffly, if desired, but they should still have ripe red strawberries as the final flourish at the top. Frozen rhubarb may be used for this if fresh rhubarb is not available.

Jack Lirio Cooking School
Jack Lirio
San Francisco, California

Serves 8
Preheat oven to 350 degrees

2 pounds fresh rhubarb
1⅛ to 1¼ cups sugar
3 pints strawberries
1 envelope plain gelatin
1 cup heavy cream

Wash the rhubarb, trim and discard the ends, and cut the stalks into 1-inch pieces. Spread the pieces in a glass baking dish and sprinkle 1 cup of the sugar over them. Cover the dish with foil and put it in the preheated oven. After 20 minutes, stir the rhubarb and then re-cover it and bake for a further 10 minutes, or until the rhubarb is tender. Let it cool, then puree it in a blender.

Rinse the strawberries under cold running water, then choose 8 of the nicest ones and reserve them for decoration. Puree 3 cups of the strawberries in a blender or food processor. Loosely chop the rest of them, and reserve. Put 2 tablespoons of the strawberry puree in a small dish and sprinkle the gelatin over it. Stir to mix and leave for a few minutes. Put the rest of the strawberry puree in a saucepan and heat, nearly to the boiling point. Add 2 to 4 tablespoons of the sugar, depending on the sweetness of the strawberries. Stir over moderate heat to dissolve the sugar, then remove from the heat and stir in the gelatin mixture. Process the strawberry mixture with 2 cups of the rhubarb puree, then add the heavy cream and blend well. Pour into a bowl and place in the freezer overnight.

When nearly ready to serve, remove the bowl from the freezer and leave at room temperature for about 10 minutes. Put the frozen mixture by spoonfuls into the food processor and blend, in batches, until smooth. Pour into chilled wine glasses or parfait glasses a little at a time, alternating with the reserved chopped strawberries and with the rest of the rhubarb puree to form layers, ending with a spoonful of the frozen mousse. On top of each place a strawberry, point up, and serve at once.

Sweet Cheese Puffs

These can be frozen, then reheated in a preheated moderate oven for about five minutes, cooled slightly, then sprinkled with confectioners' sugar.

Flo Braker
Palo Alto, California

Makes 2½ to 3 dozen pastries
Preheat oven to 375 degrees

PASTRY:
2 cups all-purpose flour
½ teaspoon salt
1 cup unsalted butter, chilled
½ cup sour cream
1 egg yolk

FILLING:
8 ounces cream cheese, at room temperature
1 egg
½ cup sugar
1 teaspoon vanilla extract
1 teaspoon finely grated lemon zest

Confectioners' sugar for sprinkling

Combine the flour and salt in a mixing bowl. Cut the butter into small pieces, and blend into the flour mixture with a pastry blender or two knives until the mixture forms into particles the size of very small peas. Combine the sour cream and the egg yolk and stir with a fork into the flour mixture. Make the pastry into a ball with the hands.

Divide the dough in half, and shape each half into a flat disk about 8 inches in diameter. Cover with plastic wrap and refrigerate overnight, or for at least 4 hours.

Combine the filling ingredients and blend until smooth.

Roll out one of the pastry disks on a lightly floured board to slightly less than ⅛-inch thickness. Cut the pastry into 3-inch squares, using a ruler, and trim off the ragged edges. Lay the squares across the round tops of ungreased miniature muffin tins measuring 1½ inches across and ¾ inch deep. Place a heaping teaspoon of filling on each square, simultaneously easing the pastry squares down into the cups. Bring opposite corners of each square to the center and press together lightly. Chill for 30 minutes.

Bake the chilled pastries in the lower third of the preheated oven for 25 to 30 minutes, until lightly browned. Cool slightly, then remove from the muffin tins and cool on racks. Sprinkle with confectioners' sugar just before serving.

Almond Gaufrettes

These cookies may be served plain, or filled with ice cream – vanilla and coffee are both good – or raspberry sorbet.

Cuisine Renaissance
Emily Didier
Napa, California

Makes 2 dozen cookies
Preheat oven to 350 degrees
Grease 2 baking sheets or line them with
    parchment paper

1¼ cups butter
1¼ cups sugar
¾ tablespoon honey
1 cup cream
5 cups coarsely ground almonds

In a heavy pan, preferably one made of copper, combine the butter, sugar, honey and ½ cup of the cream. Bring to a boil and continue cooking, stirring, for about 3 minutes. Add the almonds and remaining cream. Cook for about 3 minutes longer, stirring constantly.

Pour the mixture into a bowl to cool.

Drop tablespoonfuls of the mixture onto baking sheets, placing the spoonfuls about 5 inches apart to allow for spreading. Flatten them slightly with a fork dipped in water.

Bake in the preheated oven 5 to 7 minutes, until medium brown in color. Remove from the oven and allow to stand for about 3 to 5 minutes. Remove each one from the pan with a spatula, and roll quickly around a clean wooden broomstick or a cannoli mold.

If the cookies become too crisp to remove from the baking sheet, put them back in the oven briefly, then try again.

Chocolate Madeleines

These should be stored in airtight containers. They may be frozen.

Shirley Rubinstein
Cinnaminson, New Jersey

Makes 18 madeleines
Preheat oven to 400 degrees
Grease madeleine forms for 18 madeleines

2 large eggs
½ cup sugar
¼ cup unsweetened cocoa
1 teaspoon baking powder
¼ teaspoon salt
2 teaspoons vanilla extract
8 tablespoons unsalted butter, melted
¾ cup flour
Confectioners' sugar for dusting

Beat the eggs well in a large bowl; add the sugar and continue beating until well mixed. Add the cocoa, baking powder, salt, vanilla and melted butter, and beat for 1 minute. Sift the flour into the bowl and beat the mixture for about half a minute longer, until all the ingredients are combined.

Spoon the mixture into the madeleine forms and level the tops. Bake in the preheated oven 10 to 12 minutes, or until slightly cracked. Remove immediately from the pans and place on racks. When cool, dust with confectioners' sugar.

Coeur à la Crème with Two Sauces

Bobbi and Carole's Cooking School
Miami, Florida

Serves 8

8 ounces cream cheese, at room temperature
½ cup confectioners' sugar
Pinch of salt
1 teaspoon vanilla extract
2 cups heavy cream

CHERRY SAUCE:
1 can pitted dark cherries
1 cup red currant jelly
1½ tablespoons kirsch
1 tablespoon brandy (optional)

RASPBERRY SAUCE:
2 packages (10 ounces each) frozen
    raspberries, thawed
2 tablespoons cornstarch
½ cup red currant jelly

In a mixer, beat the cream cheese until fluffy. Blend in the sugar and salt, and add the vanilla.

In another bowl, whip the cream until stiff and add to the mixture in the mixer bowl. Blend thoroughly.

Wring out a piece of cheesecloth in ice water and spread it out. Form the cheese mixture, by hand, into a ball. Place it in the center of the cheesecloth and wrap it up. Put it in a coeur mold or a sieve and let drain over a bowl overnight in the refrigerator.

Make the cherry sauce: Drain the cherries and put their liquid in a saucepan over high heat. Reduce by boiling rapidly to about one-third the original amount. Add the jelly and cook until melted. Remove from the heat. Let cool and add the cherries, kirsch and brandy (if including). Stir.

Make the raspberry sauce: Pour the liquid from the raspberries into a measuring cup, and add enough water to make 2 cups. Put in a saucepan and add the cornstarch. Heat, stirring to blend, and let boil for 5 minutes. Stir in the jelly and heat until melted. Remove from the heat and add the raspberries.

To serve, unmold the coeur a la crème onto a serving plate and offer the two sauces to accompany it.

Cream Cheese Bavarian with Chocolate-Covered Strawberries

For this recipe, buy three pints of strawberries and sort through them carefully, separating one pint of the largest ones, of uniform size, for dipping.

Sheila Gordon
Hillsborough, California

Serves 8 to 10

¾ cup sugar
1 envelope unflavored gelatin
8 ounces cream cheese, at room temperature
1½ cups half-and-half
2 tablespoons lemon juice
1 tablespoon orange juice
1 teaspoon vanilla extract
1 tablespoon port wine

SAUCE:
2 pints strawberries
¼ to ½ cup sugar
½ teaspoon vanilla extract
1 to 2 tablespoons orange juice
1 to 2 tablespoons port wine

6 ounces semi-sweet chocolate
1 pint strawberries of uniform size

Put the sugar and gelatin in a saucepan and add ⅞ cup water. Stir to dissolve the gelatin. Bring to a boil, stirring constantly. Remove from the heat and immediately pour the mixture into a blender or food processor. Add the cream cheese, half-and-half, lemon and orange juices, vanilla and port. Blend well.

Line a glass pie plate smoothly with plastic wrap, pour in the mixture and refrigerate overnight, or for at least 6 hours.

Make the sauce: Chop the strawberries, and combine with the remaining sauce ingredients, stirring together well.

Melt the chocolate in the top of a double boiler, and dip the carefully selected strawberries in the chocolate. Chill.

To serve, unmold the Bavarian onto a round platter, discarding the plastic wrap. Place the chocolate-covered strawberries in a ring around it, and pass the sauce separately.

Chocolate Mousse-Soufflé

This dessert can be either a soufflé or a mousse. If placed in a soufflé dish and refrigerated, the decision on whether to serve it baked as a soufflé or cold as a mousse may be made close to serving time.

Richard Grausman
New York, New York

Makes 4 soufflé servings or 6 mousse servings
For soufflé, preheat oven to 475 degrees and
   butter and sugar a 4-cup soufflé dish

4 ounces semi-sweet chocolate
4 tablespoons unsalted butter
4 eggs, separated
Confectioners' sugar for sprinkling
   (for soufflé only)

  Put the chocolate and butter in a saucepan and melt over low heat. Remove from the heat and add the 4 egg yolks. Stir until the mixture thickens. Pour into a large mixing bowl.

  Beat the 4 egg whites until stiff and fold in half of the whites with a whisk, then add the other half with a rubber spatula. Pour into a soufflé dish, a serving bowl or individual cups or glasses, and refrigerate.

  For a mousse, serve after chilling for 2 hours.

  If a soufflé is preferred, bring to room temperature, then bake in the preheated oven for 5 minutes. Reduce heat to 425 degrees and bake another 5 minutes. Sprinkle with confectioners' sugar and serve immediately.

Maple Nut Bars

Maxine Horowitz
Maplewood, New Jersey

Makes 25 bars
Preheat oven to 300 degrees
Grease a 9-inch square baking pan

8 tablespoons unsalted butter,
   at room temperature
½ cup firmly packed light brown sugar
1 cup flour
2 cups broken walnuts
1 cup sugar
4 egg whites
½ teaspoon maple flavoring

  Cream the butter with the brown sugar. Add the flour and mix until smooth. Press the mixture into the baking pan, completely covering the bottom. Bake in the preheated oven for 20 minutes.

  Meanwhile place the walnuts, sugar, egg whites and maple flavoring in a small saucepan and cook over low heat for about 5 minutes, stirring occasionally, until the mixture thickens.

  Remove the baking pan from the oven, and increase the oven temperature to 350 degrees. Let the pastry cool slightly, then spoon the walnut mixture over it, spreading evenly. Return the baking pan to the oven and bake 20 minutes longer. Cool and cut into squares.

Orange and Blue-Vein Cheese Mousse

A slightly sweet but crisp Riesling will complement this mousse perfectly.

Diana R. Todd
Newport Beach, California

Serves 6

½ cup dry white wine
1½ envelopes gelatin
8 ounces cream cheese, at room temperature
6 ounces blue-vein cheese, at room temperature
¾ cup orange juice
1 teaspoon grated zest of orange
1¼ cups heavy cream
1 cup sliced fresh fruit or berries

Warm the wine and dissolve the gelatin in it.
Combine the two cheeses and the orange juice. Beat until smooth. Add the gelatin mixture and zest. Mix well.
Whip the cream until slightly thickened. Fold in.
Spoon the mixture into a 5-cup ring mold and chill until set. To serve, unmold onto a round platter, and fill the center of the ring with pieces of fresh fruit.

Sweet Avocado Pie

Bain-Marie Cooking School
Dolly Hlava
Pearland, Texas

Serves 8

1 cup mashed ripe avocado
1 cup sour cream
1¼ cups sugar
½ cup lemon juice
½ cup pineapple juice
½ cup fresh orange juice
¼ teaspoon almond extract
1 9-inch graham cracker pie crust, frozen

Combine the avocado and sour cream in a blender and mix well. Add a little of the sugar and blend, then a little of each of the juices and blend. Repeat the process until all the sugar and juices are used. Add the almond extract and blend.
Press the mixture through a strainer into the frozen pie shell and freeze overnight. Remove from the freezer about 10 minutes before serving.

Rum Caramel Mousse

This dessert may be made a day in advance, but should not be decorated earlier than an hour or two before serving.

La Belle Pomme Cooking School at Lazarus
Betty Rosbottom
Columbus, Ohio

Serves 8 to 10

1½ tablespoons gelatin
5 tablespoons dark rum
3 egg yolks
1¾ cups sugar
1½ tablespoons cornstarch
3 cups milk, scalded
2½ cups heavy cream, whipped

Combine the gelatin and rum in a small bowl and leave for a few minutes. With an electric mixer, beat the egg yolks and gradually add ¾ cup of the sugar until the mixture is thickened and light in color. Add the cornstarch and beat in slowly. Gradually add the scalded milk in a thin stream, while still beating at moderate speed. Pour the mixture into the top of a double boiler over simmering water, and heat until the mixture thickens enough to coat the back of a spoon. Stir in the rum and gelatin mixture and remove from heat. Cool slightly, then refrigerate, until chilled, stirring frequently.

Put the remaining 1 cup of sugar in a small heavy saucepan with ½ cup of water. Stir to dissolve. Cook without stirring over moderately high heat 10 to 15 minutes, until the mixture turns the color of strong tea. Pour it onto a cool oiled surface and let harden. Break into pieces and then grind it into a powder with a food processor or a mortar and pestle.

When the mousse mixture has completely cooled, remove from the refrigerator and fold in a little more than half the whipped cream and three-quarters of the caramel powder. Pour into a 3-quart soufflé dish or 8 individual 1-cup soufflé dishes. Refrigerate overnight or for several hours, until firm. Decorate the top with piped rosettes of the remaining whipped cream and sprinklings of the rest of the caramel powder.

Trifle

From France, a very English recipe. Along with shortbread and toad-in-the-hole, trifle is part of every English childhood.

École de Cuisine la Varenne
Anne Willan and Gregory Usher
Paris, France

Serves 6

CUSTARD:
3 cups milk
1 vanilla bean, split, or 1 teaspoon
   vanilla extract
4 eggs
5 egg yolks
¾ cup sugar

1 pound sponge cake or pound cake
6 ounces raspberry jam
½ cup sherry
1 pound sliced canned pears and
   peaches
1 cup heavy cream, whipped stiffly
¼ cup whole almonds, blanched and toasted

Prepare the custard: Scald the milk with the vanilla bean, if using, and leave in a warm place for 10 to 15 minutes. Beat the 4 whole eggs together with the 5 yolks and the sugar, until light and fairly thick. Stir in half the warm milk and stir this mixture back into the pan with the remaining milk in it. Heat gently, stirring constantly, until the custard thickens to the point where it will coat a spoon, taking care not to bring it to a boil, or the custard might curdle. Remove from heat at once and strain into a bowl. Add the vanilla extract if the bean was not used. Cool the custard to room temperature.

Cut the cake horizontally into three layers. Spread raspberry jam on the bottom and middle layer as you stack them. Cut into 1-inch squares. Put the squares in a 1½-quart glass bowl, spoon the sherry over them and press down lightly. Add the fruit.

Pour the custard over the fruit and cake to mask them completely. Cover the bowl and chill.

Before serving, decorate the custard with small rosettes of the stiffly whipped cream, piped from a pastry bag fitted with a star tube. Alternatively, the cream can be piped into a lattice design so the custard shows through, with rosettes around the edges. Decorate the rosettes with the toasted almonds.

Fresh Blueberry Soufflé

Those fortunate enough to possess a blueberry patch and a food processor can pick their own berries to use, either fresh or home-frozen, for this flourless soufflé.

Jane Salzfass Freiman
Chicago, Illinois

Serves 4
Preheat oven to 450 degrees

½ pound fresh or frozen blueberries, rinsed
11 tablespoons sugar
1 tablespoon butter
4 egg whites
⅛ teaspoon cream of tartar
Confectioners' sugar for decoration

Insert the metal knife blade in the container of a food processor. Process to puree the blueberries for 20 seconds. With the machine running, pour ¼ cup of the sugar through the food chute within 10 seconds.

Generously coat a 4-cup soufflé dish with butter. Sprinkle 3 tablespoons of sugar over the butter; tap out the excess sugar.

Fill a baking pan with water to a height of about an inch, making sure the soufflé dish will be able to fit into it without causing the water to overflow the pan. Place the baking pan in the oven, in the lowest position.

Beat the egg whites with the cream of tartar until soft peaks form. Continue beating, adding sugar gradually, but not beating so long that the peaks become stiff. Fold the blueberry mixture into the egg whites, and pour the combined mixture into the prepared soufflé dish. Smooth the top of the soufflé with a spatula to make it level with the top of the dish.

Place the soufflé dish carefully into the water in the baking pan and bake for 20 to 25 minutes, until the soufflé is puffed and browned. Remove from the oven and sprinkle with powdered sugar. Serve immediately.

Chocolate Walnut Pie

This is a dark, silky pie with a buttery crust. Take care with the timing — if overbaked, the filling will be too firm; on the other hand, if underbaked, it will be too runny. Serve with whipped cream.

Culinary Center of New York
Martin Johner and Gary Goldberg
New York, New York

Makes one 9-inch pie
Preheat oven to 425 degrees

CRUST:
1¾ cups flour
⅛ teaspoon salt
10 tablespoons butter, chilled,
   cut in half-inch cubes
2 tablespoons solid vegetable shortening,
   chilled
½ cup ice water
1 egg, lightly beaten

FILLING:
8 tablespoons butter
2 ounces unsweetened baking chocolate,
   coarsely chopped
1 cup light brown sugar, firmly packed
½ cup sugar
1 tablespoon flour
2 eggs
2 tablespoons milk
1 teaspoon vanilla extract
1 cup (4 ounces) coarsely chopped walnuts

Make the pastry dough: Place the flour and salt in the bowl of a food processor fitted with the steel blade. Add chilled bits of butter and shortening, and process until the butter is about the size of large peas. Add the ice water and process just until the dough begins to come together on the blades.

(Do not let the dough form a ball in the processor.)

Remove the dough from the processor and shape quickly into a ball. Cut in half and form two equal-sized balls. Lightly flour each ball, wrap in plastic wrap and chill for at least 2 hours. (The dough will keep for a month in the freezer, wrapped well.)

Butter the inside surface of a 9-inch pie tin. Place one ball of dough on a lightly floured pastry cloth or board. Beat the chilled dough several times with a rolling pin to soften it.

Roll the dough into a circle about 2 inches larger in diameter than the mold and ⅛-inch thick. Fold the circle over itself twice, into quarters, and position the point at the center of the pie tin; unfold. Smooth it, lift the edges of the dough to settle into the mold and trim and flute the edge. Prick the shell with a fork at ½-inch intervals. Refrigerate for at least half an hour before prebaking. Butter a sheet of aluminum foil and set it, butter-side down, in the chilled pastry shell, pressing the foil gently up around the sides. Weight the shell with dried beans or rice, and bake for 12 to 15 minutes in a low position in the preheated oven. Remove the beans or rice and the aluminum liner and brush the pastry with the beaten egg; bake 5 minutes, then remove the shell from the pie tin and let cool completely on a rack before returning it to the pie tin to be filled.

Reset the oven to 325 degrees.

Melt butter and chocolate in a heavy-bottomed saucepan over moderate heat, stirring constantly. Do not let it burn.

Remove from the heat and immediately add both the sugars, and the flour. Mix well. Beat in the eggs, milk and vanilla. Scatter the chopped walnuts on the bottom of the pastry shell and carefully pour the chocolate mixture over them. Bake for 40 to 45 minutes, just until the top forms a crust. Cool to serve at room temperature (do not refrigerate).

Fondant

This is a basic fondant, smooth and easy to make. It can have flavoring added at the end, or nuts, cherries or the like, then be formed into balls and dipped in chocolate to make chocolate cream candies.

Country Kitchen
Mildred Brand
Fort Wayne, Indiana

Makes cream centers for about 125 small candies

5 cups sugar
1 cup milk
1 cup heavy cream
4 tablespoons butter
½ teaspoon cream of tartar

Combine the sugar, milk, cream, butter and cream of tartar in a large saucepan. Place over high heat. Bring to a boil, then put a candy thermometer into the boiling syrup. Cook, stirring only occasionally, and lowering the heat gradually as the mixture thickens, until the temperature reaches 236 degrees. Pour out onto baking sheets or a marble slab, and cool to lukewarm. Work with a spatula until the fondant creams up into a semi-solid mass. Knead with the hands until smooth before forming into balls. Let rest on the slab until completely cool.

ALABAMA

Bonnie Bailey Cooking Classes
Bonnie Bailey
Birmingham, AL

Phyllis S. Browne
Tuscaloosa, AL

Kitchen Things, Inc.
Lenore Picard
Birmingham, AL

★ Seasonal Kitchen
Jean Sparks
Huntsville, AL

ARIZONA

C. Steele and Co.
Carol Steele
Scottsdale, AZ

Barbara A. Colleary
Tempe, AZ

★ Donald S. Luria
Tucson, AZ

Parisian Kitchen, Ltd.
Ann Thomas Hand
Tucson, AZ

★ The Tasting Spoon
Maryellen Thoman
Tucson, AZ

ARKANSAS

★ Sally Flanzer
Little Rock, AR

CALIFORNIA

Sandra Nair Allen
Santa Barbara, CA

Karen J. Berk
Tarzana, CA

★ Lenore Bleadon
Kentfield, CA

★ Flo Braker
Palo Alto, CA

Biba Caggiano
Sacramento, CA

California Culinary Academy
Danielle Carlisle, Ron Batori
San Francisco, CA

Cantonese Gourmet
  Cooking School
Rose Chang Alexander
San Francisco, CA

Hugh Carpenter
Santa Barbara, CA

★ Charcuterie Cooking School
  of Food & Wine
Scottie McKinney, Gayle DiKellis
Sausalito, CA

Tillie Clements
China Hills, CA

Cookery at the Cove
Jack Schneider, Ed Borowiec
Ovinda, CA

★ Creative Cuisinières
    Frazier Farms Cooking School
Kathie Frazier, Amy Wandalowski
Escondido, CA

★ Cuisine Renaissance
Carole Patton
Napa, CA

Martha Culbertson
Fallbrook, CA

Patricia Derdivanis
Oakland, CA

Carolyn Dille
Menlo Park, CA

★ Joanne Donsky
San Francisco, CA

Mary Jane Drinkwater
Berkeley, CA

Theodora Duvall
Del Mar, CA

Fassaro's International School
  of Cooking
Linda Fassaro
Corona Del Mar, CA

Merren B. Forsgren
Sacramento, CA

Jean Fortenbery
Palo Alto, CA

Lonnie Gandara
San Francisco, CA

Eileen Gillespie
Escondido, CA

Gerri Gilliland
Santa Monica, CA

Good Cooks & Co.
Arlene Brennan Day
Palo Alto, CA

★ Sheila Gordon
Hillsborough, CA

Martha Green
Redlands, CA

Antonia Allegra Griffin
San Diego, CA

Lillian Haines, C.E.C.
Beverly Hills, CA

★ Hayward School of Cookery
  & Catering
Geraldean Hayward
Los Angeles, CA

Jean Hensman
Escondido, CA

Sharon Tyler Herbst
San Rafael, CA

Janice M. Herwick
Tiburon, CA

Rosemary Hinton-Barron
San Francisco, CA

Virginia A. Hjelte
Walnut Creek, CA

Mable Hoffman
Solana Beach, CA

Ken Hom
Berkeley, CA

Inner Gourmet Cooking School
Peggy Rahn, Sue Kranwinkle
Pasadena, CA

★ Jack Lirio Cooking School
Jack Lirio
San Francisco, CA

Fran Jenkins
Rancho Santa Fe, CA

Josephine Gatan
  Cooking School
Josephine Gatan Shiplacoff
Los Angeles, CA

Joyce Jue
San Francisco, CA

Terri Julio
Arcadia, CA

★ Loni Kuhn
San Francisco, CA

★ Sharon W. Lane
Irvine, CA

Le Cordon Rouge
Jay Perkins
San Rafael, CA

Le Kookery
Mitzie Cutler
Sherman Oaks, CA

★ Lesand's
  Louise Fiszer
Menlo Park, CA

Marlene Levinson
San Francisco, CA

Evie Lieb
Carmichael, CA

Dorothy Louie
Oakland, CA

Ma Cuisine
Wolfgang Puck, Patrick Terrail,
  Judy Gethers
Los Angeles, CA

Rosemary Manell
Belvedere, CA

Ellie Manser
Los Altos, CA

★ Marlene Sorosky's
  Cooking Center
Marlene Sorosky
Tarzana, CA

Raymond G. Marshall
Pasadena, CA

Paul H. Mayer, Jr.
San Francisco, CA

Sharon Meresman
Los Altos, CA

★ Microwave Cooking Center, Inc.
Thelma Pressman
Encino, CA

★ Carlo Middione
San Francisco, CA

Mission Gourmet
  Cooking School
Mary Chamberlin, Kathy Tabke
Fremont, CA

Montana Mercantile
Rachel Cronin
Santa Monica, CA

Thomas R. Newman
San Francisco, CA

★ Donna Nordin
San Francisco, CA

Marjorie Nyrop
Los Angeles, CA

★ Anne Otterson
La Jolla, CA

The Perfect Pan
George Munger
San Diego, CA

Phyllis Ann Marshall
  Cooking School
Phyllis Ann Marshall
Orange, CA

★ Contributors to this book

CALIFORNIA

Noma Pinto
San Diego, CA

Marge Poore
Novato, CA

Kittina Powers
San Rafael, CA

Belle Rhodes
Rutherford, CA

Marcie Rothman
Los Angeles, CA

Santa Barbara Cooking School
Barbara Sims-Bell
Santa Barbara, CA

Gabrielle M. Saylor
San Mateo, CA

Teruko Shimizu
Sunnyvale, CA

Grant W. Showley
Irvine, CA

Dawn Marie Simms
Walnut Creek, CA

★ Susan Slack
Mission Viejo, CA

Something More
Sarah Williamson
La Mesa, CA

Lois W. Stanton
Del Mar, CA

Jerrie Strom
Rancho Santa Fe, CA

Thayer Tischler Taft
La Mesa, CA

Tante Marie's Cooking School
Mary Risley
San Francisco, CA

★ Elizabeth V. Thomas
Berkeley, CA

Virginia S. Thomas
La Jolla, CA

★ Diana Todd
Newport Beach, CA

Barbara Tropp
San Francisco, CA

Nancy A. Velasquez
Fresno, CA

Virtuoso
Theodore S. Cohen
Terra Linda, CA

★ Von Welanetz Cooking Workshop
Diana & Paul Von Welanetz
Pacific Palisades, CA

Walbert & Co.'s
 "Cook School in the Loft"
Rosemary K. Walbert
Encino, CA

★ What's Cooking
Bill Kuretich
Torrance, CA

What's Cooking Restaurant
Lucy Ann Luhan
Newport Beach, CA

Grace L. Wheeler
La Jolla, CA

Lois P. Whitworth
Fresno, CA

Janis D. Wicks
Walnut Creek, CA

William Glen Cooking School
Suzanne Keller-Peterson
Sacramento, CA

Pamela Wischkaemper
San Francisco, CA

★ Kenneth C. Wolfe
Lafayette, CA

Martin M. Yan
Davis, CA

Rhoda Yee
Walnut Creek, CA

COLORADO

★ Helen Augustine
Golden, CO

★ Chez Deborah
Deborah Mefferd
Evergreen, CO

★ Cookery & Company
Pat Miller, Edie Acsell
Englewood, CO

The Little Kitchen
Judy Bell
Colorado Springs, CO

Patricia Morrison
Colorado Springs, CO

Peppercorn Gourmet Goods
 and Cooking School, Inc.
Barbara David, D. Houghland
Boulder, CO

Kay Pitcher
Vail, CO

★ World of Cuisine
Marcia R. Fox
Denver, CO

CONNECTICUT

Ann Howard Cookery, Ltd.
Ann Howard
Farmington, CT

★ Beverly Cox
Southport, CT

Marjorie P. Blanchard
Greens Farms, CT

The Complete Kitchen, Inc.
Mary Murray
Darien, CT

The Culinary Arts
Cecile Rivel
Wilton, CT

Nancy B. Mott
Greenwich, CT

Julie A. Pennella
Riverside, CT

★ Constance Quan
Old Greenwich, CT

★ The Silo
Ruth Henderson
New Milford, CT

DELAWARE

The Cooking School at
 the Kitchen Cupboard
Debbie Flayhart
Dover, DE

★ Patricia Tabibian
Wilmington, DE

DISTRICT OF COLUMBIA

★ David Robert Berger
Washington, DC

★ Mario Cardullo
Washington, DC

Carol Cutler
Washington, DC

★ Kitchen Bazaar
Alan Shefter, Sherman Shapiro,
 Barbara Jeffress
Washington, DC

Carol Mason
Washington, DC

Elizabeth Warren-Smith
Washington, DC

FLORIDA

Marie Bass (S/A)
Lakeland, FL

★ Bobbi & Carole's Cooking School
Bobbi Garber, Carole Kotkin
Miami, FL

Deborah Carrow
Clearwater, FL

★ Sue Sutker's Creative Cookery,
 Maas Brothers
Sue Sutker
Tampa, FL

Cuisine Classics Cooking School
Sally Fine
Sarasota, FL

Mimi Hartman
Longwood, FL

★ Marla Horn
Hollywood, FL

★ Myrle Horn
Hollywood, FL

Maryalice LaForest
Treasure Island, FL

Mary Stames King's
 Cooking School
Mary Stames King
Destin, FL

Francois Metraux
Miami, FL

Claire Moderelli
Tampa, FL

Peggy O'Donnell
Land O'Lakes, FL

Kathleen Perry
Longwood, FL

★ Marina Polvay
Miami Shores, FL

Pot 'n' Pan Tree
Bebe L. Corson
Palm Beach, FL

"The School" at Bon Appetit
Eve Montella, Michael &
 Paula Finkle
Plantation, FL

★ Sara E. Sharpe
Miami, FL

★ Dorothy Sims
Tampa, FL

Someone's in the Kitchen
 with Mimi
Mimi Kersun
Jacksonville, FL

The Unpressured Cooker
Linda Uhler
Fort Myers, FL

GEORGIA

★ Barbara H. Brown
Roswell, GA

Cook's Corner, Inc.
Brenda M. Hodges
Atlanta, GA

★ Shirley O. Corriher
Atlanta, GA

★ Nathalie Dupree
Atlanta, GA

★ Doris Koplin
Atlanta, GA

★ Bailee Kronowitz
Savannah, GA

Christiane J. LeGuen
Atlanta, GA

★ Frances Neel
White, GA

★ Peggy Foreman's Cooking School
Peggy Foreman
Atlanta, GA

★ Alice Copeland Phillips
Atlanta, GA

Susan Puett
Atlanta, GA

★ Deen Terry
Atlanta, GA

★ Ursula's Cooking School
Ursula Knaeusel
Atlanta, GA

★ Diane Wilkinson
Atlanta, GA

★ Roxanna Young
Atlanta, GA

HAWAII

★ Creative Cookery, Ltd.
LaVonne S. Tollerud
Honolulu, HI

ILLINOIS

★ Nancy L. Abrams
Evanston, IL

★ Jane Armstrong
Melrose Park, IL

Helen Baetz
Barrington, IL

S. Maria Battaglia
Evanston, IL

★ Judith Bell
Chicago, IL

★ Cynthia Berland
Chicago, IL

Pasquale Bruno
Chicago, IL

★ Madelaine D. Bullwinkel
Hinsdale, IL

Charie's Kitchen
Charie MacDonald
Wilmette, IL

Charlene S. Cohen
Niles, IL

The Complete Cook
Wilma Sugarman, Elaine Sherman
Deerfield, IL

Foodstuffs, Inc.
Carole Segal
Glencoe, IL

★ Jane Salzfass Freiman
Chicago, IL

Patty Godfrey
Ottawa, IL

★ Rosaleah Goland
Skokie, IL

Elaine Gonzalez
Northbrook, IL

★ Monique Jamet Hooker
Wilmette, IL

J & D Marketing/
Cooking with Class
Joan & David O'Bryant
Champaign, IL

Maria B. Kijac
Lincoln Shire, IL

★ Nancy Kirby
Lake Bluff, IL

Lois Carol Levine
Chicago, IL

Joan C. Loyd
Deerfield, IL

★ Microcookery Center, Inc.
Mary Jo Bergland
Glen Ellyn, IL

★ Pat Opler
Hinsdale, IL

★ Oriental Food Market &
Cooking School
Pansy & Chu-Yen Luke
Chicago, IL

Marsha Lee Pener
Chicago, IL

The Persimmon Tree
Bill & Jane Briner, Ellen Ewing
Geneva, IL

★ Barbara Pisik
Deerfield, IL

The Proper Pan, Inc.
Cynthia Schmitt
Peoria, IL

Quincy Steamboat Co.
Mary M. Kube
Quincy, IL

Connie C. Riherd
Flossmoor, IL

Bertie Selinger
Mt. Prospect, IL

Ginny Shelton
Naperville, IL

★ Falicia Slavik
Mt. Prospect, IL

Lois Calhoun Smith
Rockford, IL

Paula A. Solinger
Hinsdale, IL

Carolyn Sue Spitler
Chicago, IL

Sunnyside Up
Diane Olson
Rockford, IL9

Barbara Tuleja
Palos Park, IL

Jill Van Cleave
Chicago, IL

Judith Vance
La Grange, IL

★ Shirley Waterloo
Hinsdale, IL

★ What's Cooking
Ruth Law
Hinsdale, IL

Wilton School of Cake Decorating
and Confectionary Arts
Zella Junkin, Manuel Lopez
Woodridge, IL

INDIANA

★ The Clay Kitchen at the East Bank
Norma Singleton
South Bend, IN

Bernard Clayton, Jr.
Bloomington, IN

★ Country Kitchen
Mildred Brand
Fort Wayne, IN

★ Dorothy Crebo
Kokomo, IN

Cuisine Unlimited, Inc.
Beverly J. Badowich
Merrillville, IN

★ The Eight Mice Cooking School
Joanne Force, Tee Montfort
Lafayette, IN

Great Cooks & Co.
Mary Ellen Davies
Indianapolis, IN

★ Judith Goldinger
Schererville, IN

IOWA

★ Chez Mimi Cooking School
Mimi Gormezano
Iowa City, IA

Dixie Fishbaugh
Shenandoah, IA

Hanna E. Runge
Davenport, IA

KANSAS

The Back Burner
Rick & Heidi Allen
Overland Park, KS

Phyllis J. Brock
Overland Park, KS

Phyllis Nason
Lake Quivira, KS

★ Bobbi Saper
Shawnee Mission, KS

Polly Q. Spencer
Topeka, KS

KENTUCKY

Nancy Bailey
Prospect, KY

Helen L. Lang
Louisville, KY

★ Lillian Marshall's School for Cooks
Lillian Marshall
Louisville, KY

LOUISIANA

Cooking, Inc.
Terry L. Thompson
Lafayette, LA

Marilyn Farrow
Luling, LA

★ Lee Barnes Cooking School
Lee Barnes
New Orleans, LA

The New Orleans School of Cooking
Joseph S. Cahn
New Orleans, LA

Toute de Suite á la Microwave, Inc.
Jean Durkee
Lafayette, LA

J.C. Whitfield
Oil City, LA

Wok & Whisk, Inc.
Barbara & Dan Peterson
Baton Rouge, LA

MAINE

★ Mead Brownell
Freeport, ME

★ Beryl Marton
Ogunquit, ME

Suzanne Taylor
East Blue Hill, ME

The Whip and Spoon
Sonia B. Robertson
Portland, ME

MARYLAND

Leslie E. Bloom
Silver Spring, MD

Linda W. Brown
Baltimore, MD

Rona Cohen
Bethesda, MD

★ Lee R. Ehudin
Lutherville, MD

★ Elaine B. Forman
Potomac, MD

Sheilah Kaufman
Potomac, MD

★ L'Academie de Cuisine
Francois Dionot
Bethesda, MD

Shelley P. Levi
Bethesda, MD

Sandra M. Naumann
Accident, MD

Vivian Samuelian Portner
Silver Spring, MD

Germaine Sharretts
Baltimore, MD

Ginger Silvers
Potomac, MD

★ What's Cooking!
Phyllis Frucht
Rockville, MD

MASSACHUSETTS

Margie Beller Borenstein
West Newton, MA

Julia Child
Cambridge, MA

Creative Cuisine
Roberta Dowling
Cambridge, MA

Ethel Goralnick's Elegant Cuisine
Ethel Goralnick
Haverhill, MA

June Gosule
Weston,MA

Sheryl Julian
Watertown, MA

Jane Heald Lavine
Brookline, MA

Modern Gourmet Boston
Polly Yates
Newton Centre, MA

Modern Gourmet, Inc.
Madeleine M. Kamman
Newton Centre, MA

Nina Simonds
Manchester, MA

Patricia Skillman
Chestnut Hill, MA

Mary Taylor
Beverly, MA

MICHIGAN

★ Nell Benedict
Lathrup Village, MI

Judith D. Breen (S/A)
East Lansing, MI

★ Complete Cuisine
Alexandra Cooper
Ann Arbor, MI

Brigid O. Flynn (S/A)
Grosse Ile, MI

Mary Kathryn Genova
Ann Arbor, MI

Kitchen Mechanics, Inc.
Sharon Yff
Grand Haven, MI

Christine McClurg (S/A)
Flint, MI

★ Judith Martin
Port Huron, MI

The Micro Place
Kaye Cuser
Kalamazoo, MI

Trudy Modell School
of Cooking
Trudy Modell
Birmingham, MI

Michelle Niemiec (S/A)
Canton Township, MI

Maureen F. Porubsky (S/A)
Plymouth, MI

Arlene White (S/A)
Kalamazoo, MI

MINNESOTA

★ Sharon P. Baird
Edina, MN

Nancy J. Bubalo
Minneapolis, MN

★ Cinnamon Toast, Inc.
Sara & Mark Siegel
Minnetonka, MN

Marion Conlin
Minneapolis, MN

The Cookery School
Sharon Stumpf
Winona, MN

Creative Cooking, Inc.
Sharon Conlan, Bonnie Pope
White Bear Lake, MN

★ Rubye Erickson
Edina, MN

★ Lois Lee
Minneapolis, MN

Yvonne Moody
St. Paul, MN

Beatrice A. Ojakangas
Duluth, MN

Th'rice
Martha Kaemmer, Mary Lofgren
St. Paul, MN

MISSISSIPPI

Chez Cuisine, Ltd.
Carolyn Blakey, Susan Winkler
Tupelo, MS

Barbara N. Kroeze
Madison, MS

MISSOURI

Dierberg's School of Cooking
Barbara Foersterling
St. Louis, MO

★ Susan Manlin Katzman
Clayton, MO

★ Pampered Pantry
Marie Mosher
St. Louis, MO

Parisian Pantry, Ltd.
Margaret E. Pinckley
Springfield, MO

NEBRASKA

Lincoln Cooking Company
Adele Wohlers
Lincoln, NE

NEW HAMPSHIRE

★ Lynn B. Smith
Hanover, NH

NEW JERSEY

Annie's Kitchen
at Bazaar Bizarre, Inc.
Anne L. Casale
Plainfield, NJ

Cooking with Susan Rhoades
Susan G. Rhoades
Englewood, NJ

Cooktique
Silvia Lehrer
Tenafly, NJ

Jinny Dickenson
Moorestowne, NJ

Ann I. Harwood
Princeton, NJ

Yocheved Hirsch
Tenafly, NJ

★ Maxine Horowitz
Maplewood, NJ

★ Look & Cook
Bunny Dell
Teaneck, NJ

Mai Leung Classic Chinese
Cooking School
Mai Leung
Madison, NJ

Anita Prichard
Cranbury, NJ

Ellen Rochford
Tenafly, NJ

★ Shirley Rubinstein
Cinnaminson, NJ

★ The Uncomplicated Gourmet
Nancy Stem
Westwood, NJ

★ Carole Walter
Emerson, NJ

Sally Wernicoff
Ocean City, NJ

★ Jean Yueh
Summit, NJ

★ Mary Jane Zirolli
Clifton, NJ

NEW YORK

★ Donna Adams
New York, NY

Marie Agresti
Franklin Square, NY

Gail Anderson
Manlius, NY

Elizabeth Andoh
New York, NY

Miriam Brickman
New York, NY

★ Giuliano Bugialli
New York, NY

Jane Butel
New York, NY

★ Carol's Cuisine
Carol Giudice
Staten Island, NY

Russell S. Carr
New York, NY

★ Irena Chalmers
New York, NY

Ann Lee Chassen
Atlantic Beach, NY

★ Mary Beth Clark
New York, NY

★ Cordon Rose
Rose Levy Beranbaum
New York, NY

Country Kitchen Cooking School
Anita Robertson, Nancy Radke
Fayetteville, NY

★ Culinary Center of New York
Martin Johner, Gary Goldberg
New York, NY

Eileen Diffin S/A
Clay, NY

★ Richard Grausman
New York, NY

Bert Greene
New York, NY

Marcella Hazan
New York, NY

★ John Clancy's Kitchen Workshop
John Clancy
New York, NY

★ Karen Lee's Chinese
Cooking Classes
Karen Lee
New York, NY

★ Gilda Latzky
New York, NY

Liang's Chinese Cooking School
Lucille Liang
Pleasantville, NY

★ Libby Hillman's Cooking School
Libby Hillman
Great Neck, NY

Joann Lindauer
White Plains, NY

★ Beverly Margolis
Utica, NY

★ Perla Meyers
New York, NY

Rhoda Paul
Franklin Square, NY

Peter Kump's New York
Cooking School
Peter Kump
New York, NY

★ Barbara Pullo
Suffern, NY

Rosa Ross' Wok on Wheels
Rosa Ross
Brooklyn Heights, NY

Ann Rowan
North Salem, NY

Julie Sahni
Brooklyn Heights, NY

Richard Sax
New York, NY

Merle Schell
New York, NY

Blake E. Swihart
New York, NY

Marie A. Tedeschi
Pittsford, NY

Emily Tom
Jamaica, NY

Michele Urvater
New York, NY

Marcie Ver Ploeg
Pittsford, NY

Comelia E. Walmsley
Lewiston, NY

Paula Wolfert
New York, NY

Yellow Cart Cooking School
Kathleen Dublanica
New Hartford, NY

NORTH CAROLINA

★ Anne Byrd
Charlotte, NC

★ The Cook's Roost
Joanne B. Copeland
Fayetteville, NC

★ Nancy Coolidge
Fayetteville, NC

The Kitchen Cupboard
Betty Grossnickle
Greenville, NC

The Saucepan
Mary Ann Sayre
Wilmington, NC

The Stocked Pot & Co.
Janet S. Mueller
Winston-Salem, NC

Beth Tartan
Winston-Salem, NC

Kaye Warrington
Fayetteville, NC

Edwina Hardy Worth
Raleigh, NC

OHIO

Iris B. Bailin
Cleveland Heights, OH

Terry Buxton
Worthington, OH

★ The Common Market School
of Cooking
Donna Welsch
Cincinnati, OH

Good Things
Nancy Jeffery
Columbus, OH

Pamela Grosscup
Cleveland Heights, OH

★ Barbra C. Heiken
Cincinnati, OH

Beatrice D. Krakoff
Columbus, OH

★ La Belle Pomme Cooking School
at Lazarus
Betty Rosbottom
Columbus, OH

Claudia E. Sansone
Youngstowne, OH

Mary Carol Smith
Akron, OH

Bruce C. Williams
Sylvania, OH

★ Zona Spray Cooking School
Zona Spray
Hudson, OH

OKLAHOMA

Creative Cookery
Jon Orenstein
Oklahoma City, OK

Carol E. Smaglinski
Edmond, OK

OREGON

Joyce M. Barnekow
Portland, OR

Bryden's Store
Vicki Anne Bryden
Medford, OR

Carl's Cuisine
Carl Meisel
Salem, OR

★ Cloudtree & Sun
Mary Jo Hessel, Joanne Stoney
Gresham, OR

Nonie Fish
Eugene, OR

Barbara Harris
Portland, OR

Hot Pots Gourmet Cooking School
Ellie Kringer
Lincoln City, OR

John Hurst Cooking Classes
John L. Hurst
Eugene, OR

Kitchen Kaboodle
Jane Hibler
Portland, OR

★ Richard Nelson Cooking Classes
Richard Nelson
Portland, OR

★ Joanne E. Stoney
Troutdale, OR

Nancy Taylor
Portland, OR

PENNSYLVANIA

★ Charlotte Ann Albertson's
   Kitchen Saucer Cooking School
Charlotte Ann Albertson
Wynnewood, PA

Jane Citron
Pittsburgh, PA

The Cooking School at
   Waterloo Gardens
Linda LeBoutillier
Devon, PA

Creative Cooking, Inc.
Julie Dannenbaum
Philadelphia, PA

Diana Resek's School of Cooking
Diana Resek
Riegelsville, PA

Eclectic Cooking
Lou Sackett, Barbara Bergen
Philadelphia, PA

Anita Hirsch
Allentown, PA

Rosemary S. Jung
Berwyn, PA

★ Kay's School of Cookery
Kathryn Domurot
Pittsburgh, PA

★ Hermie Kranzdorf
Narberth, PA

The Restaurant School
Daniel Liberatoscioli
Philadelphia, PA

★ Marlene Parrish Teaches Cooking!
Marlene Parrish
Sewickley, PA

Mei Ling Moy
Broomall, PA

★ Joan Polin
Melrose Park, PA

★ Irene Rothschild
Elkins Park, PA

G. Parke Rouse, III
Gladwyne, PA

Bernice Sisson
Swarthmore, PA

Rita M. Stanton
Allentown, PA

★ Virginia Stefani
Pittsburgh, PA

Rose Marie Taraborrelli
Morton, PA

To Market, To Market
Irena Smith, Felicity Taormina
Philadelphia, PA

Janet Zamsky
Gladwyne, PA

PUERTO RICO

Cuisine-Cuisine
Miriam & Sonia Miranda
Pince, PR

RHODE ISLAND

Chef's Company
Nancy Barr
Providence, RI

SOUTH CAROLINA

Amelia M. Cartledge
N. Augusta, SC

★ Susan B. Langhorne
Hilton Head Island, SC

★ Marion B. Sullivan
Columbia SC

August & Evelyn Wavpotich
Hilton Head, SC

TENNESSEE

★ Cook and Company
Larry W. Brown
Nashville, TN

Cooking Unlimited
Katheleen Barron
Knoxville, TN

Forty Carrots
Frances Averitt
Memphis, TN

The Happy Baker Cooking School
Dwight & Happy Baker
Chattanooga, TN

★ Ruth H. Howse
Memphis, TN

Virginia S. Johnson
Nashville, TN

★ Gloria Olson
Nashville, TN

Thayer W. Wine
Holladay, TN

TEXAS

Lenny Angel
San Antonio, TX

★ Bain-Marie
Dolly Hlava
Pearland, TX

★ Karen D. Benner
Houston, TX

★ Sally Bernstein
Houston, TX

★ Mary Blake Bryant
Austin, TX

Ann Clark
Austin, TX

Cooking with Amber
Amber C. Robinson
Dallas, TX

Carol Dignan
Dallas, TX

Virginia T. Elverson
Houston, TX

The French Apron, Inc.
Louise Lamensdorf, Renie Steves
Fort Worth, TX

Gourmet's Kitchen
Virginia Lee Hester
Houston, TX

★ Gourmet Stop!
Laura Lempert, Phyllis Kalmin
Houston, TX

Rosanne Greene
Dallas, TX

The Happy Wok
Sara B. Aleshire
Austin, TX

Francoise Harris
Houston, TX

Karen Hilliard
Odessa, TX

★ Hilltop Herb Farm
Madalene Hill, Gwen Barclay
Cleveland, TX

Judith D. Hines
Brownwood, TX

Houston Home and Garden
   Cooking Center
Anne Fitzgerald
Houston, TX

★ Carmen Jones
Spring, TX

★ The Lemon Tree
Charlotte Kuppinger
Harlingen, TX

Patricia P. McKinney
Odessa, TX

A.W. Morriss
Tyler, TX

Mary Nell Reck
Houston, TX

Linda J. Arndt Schuelke
Houston, TX

Katherine Shane
Houston, TX

Diane Shea
Weslaco, TX

Southampton's Kitchen
Gloria and Leroy Kliebert
Houston, TX

Gloria Soto
Victoria, TX

Sue Lowe Sims
San Angelo, TX

Julia L. Thomas (S/A)
Eagle Lake, TX

VIRGINIA

James Carnevale
Arlington, VA

★ The Happy Cooking School, Inc.
Dolores Kostelni
Lexington, VA

Amy Malone
Falls Church, VA

Memory & Co. School of Cooking
Ann Memory
Charlottesville, VA

★ Potluck
Walter O. Angel
Fredericksburg, VA

John Thomas
Arlington, VA

Ann Worley
Arlington, VA

VERMONT

Culinary Center of Vermont
J.M. Clark
Stowe, VT

WASHINGTON

Judy Won Lew
Seattle, WA

★ Magnolia Kitchen Shoppe
Irma Goertzen
Seattle, WA

Christie Williams
Federal Way, WA

The Yankee Kitchen
   Cooking School
Nancy A. Lazara
Bellvue, WA

WEST VIRGINIA

Creative Cooking School at Potluck
Lavonne Sanders, Diana Amores
Charleston, WV

WISCONSIN

Bert Slawson's Cook Nook
Bert Slawson
Waukesha, WI

★ Jill Heavenrich
Milwaukee, WI

Jane Jordan
Shorewood, WI

★ Catherine Kunkle
New Richmond, WI

Le Bec Fin
Carole Grohmann
Milwaukee, WI

Diane F. McGauran
Milwaukee, WI

★ Modern Gourmet of Milwaukee
Myra Dorros
Milwaukee, WI

Barbara Kay Spring
Bayside, WI

Sylvia S. Vaccaro
Madison, WI

Linda E. Wilkerson
Milwaukee, WI

CANADA

Betty's Kitchen, Ltd.
Betty Shields
Nepean, Ontario

Bonnie Stern School of Cooking
Bonnie Stern
Toronto, Ontario

Cuisine de Barbara
Barbara Miachika
West Vancouver, BC

Cuisine Nouvelle de France, Inc.
Vivian de Boice Baker
Toronto, Ontario

Eileen Dwillies
Delta, BC

J. Johns Conservatory of World Cookery, Ltd.
Virginia J. Johns
Vancouver, BC

Kasey Wilson Cooking School
Kasey Wilson
Vancouver, BC

Norene's Cuisine
Norene Gilletz
Dollard des Ormeaux, Quebec

Yvonne Munk
Waterloo, Ontario

Mario Novati
Pointe Claire, Quebec

Susan Poulter's School of Creative Cooking
Susan Poulter
Thunder Bay, Ontario

OVERSEAS

The Cordon Bleu Cookery School (London)
Rosemary Hume
London, England

Miller Howe
John Tovey
Windermere, England

Sherrie Sorenson
London, England

Holly Towers
London, England

★ Lynne Kasper
Brussels, Belgium

★ Ecole de Cuisine La Varenne
Anne Willan, Gregory Usher
Paris, France

Le Cordon Bleu
Mme. E. Bressart
Paris, France

Anne Roberts
Paris, France

Experimental Kitchen Craft Institute
Mahinder Kapoor
Calcutta, West Bengal, India

Leah Oman
Madrid, Spain

ASSOCIATE MEMBERS

Best Foods
Englewood Cliffs, NJ

California Apricot Advisory Board
Walnut Creek, CA

Charles Jacquin et Cie.
Philadelphia, PA

Commercial Aluminum Cookware Co.
Toledo, OH

Del Monte
San Francisco, CA

Ecko Housewares
Franklin Park, IL

Farberware
Bronx, NY

Fleischmann's Div. Standard Brands, Inc.
Rochelle Park, NJ

The Maxim Company
Newark, NJ

Medaglia D'Oro Espresso Coffee
Palisades Park, NJ

Ocean Spray Cranberries, Inc.
Plymouth, MA

Pacific Pearl Seafood
Bellevue, WA

Planters, Div. Standard Brands, Inc.
Rochelle Park, NJ

Robot-Coupe International Corp.
East Norwalk, CT

Sanyo Electric Inc.
Little Ferry, NJ

The Silver Palate
New York, NY

Waring Products Division
New Hartford, CT

W.A. Taylor
Miami, FL

★ Contributors to this book

For friends who may be interested in ordering this book:

----

order   coupon

To: Irena Chalmers Cookbooks, Inc. / P.O. Box 322 / Brown Summit, NC 27214

Please send me _____ copies of the International Association of Cooking Schools
COOKBOOK. I enclose **$10.95** plus **95 cents** for postage and handling for each copy.

M _____

_____

_____ Zip _____

(North Carolina residents should add applicable tax)

----

order   coupon

To: Irena Chalmers Cookbooks, Inc. / P.O. Box 322 / Brown Summit, NC 27214

Please send me _____ copies of the International Association of Cooking Schools
COOKBOOK. I enclose **$10.95** plus **95 cents** for postage and handling for each copy.

M _____

_____

_____ Zip _____

(North Carolina residents should add applicable tax)

----

order   coupon

To: Irena Chalmers Cookbooks, Inc. / P.O. Box 322 / Brown Summit, NC 27214

Please send me _____ copies of the International Association of Cooking Schools
COOKBOOK. I enclose **$10.95** plus **95 cents** for postage and handling for each copy.

M _____

_____

_____ Zip _____

(North Carolina residents should add applicable tax)

----

*"One of the best chefs I know told
me recently, 'You know, almost every
day I learn something new.'
"I think that's the spirit we should
continue with."*

*— JULIA CHILD, addressing
cooking school teachers
March 21, 1981*